# WITH MALICE TOWARD ONE:

## A True Story of Prostitution, Politics and a Pulitzer Prize in Nevada

BY CLYDE BIGLIERI

**PUBLISHED BY:**

Ieri Books, LLC

Published by Ieri Books, LLC
P.O. Box 911
Reno, Nevada 89504

With Malice Toward One: A True Story of Prostitution, Politics and a
Pulitzer Prize in Nevada

This book is a first edition.

**For Book Orders**
The author may be contacted at P.O. Box 911, Reno, Nevada 89504 or
(775) 842-8064 (between 10 a.m. and 5 p.m. PST)
ieribooks@yahoo.com

Designed by Jessie Gardner
JG Designers, Inc.
www.jgdesigners.com

ISBN: 978-0-615-31339-9

The author is grateful for permission to include the following previously
copyrighted material:
"Real Estate Investigation Files Destroyed" in the Nevada Appeal
February 15, 1978

# WITH MALICE TOWARD ONE:
## A TRUE STORY OF PROSTITUTION, POLITICS AND A PULITZER PRIZE IN NEVADA

By Clyde Biglieri

## DEDICATION

This book is dedicated to our four daughters. As young women (girls) they witnessed and endured the humiliation and scorn heaped upon their father by the press when a grand jury in Reno, Nevada, falsely accused him of a crime, totally ignoring the 4th amendment of the U.S. Constitution and using county, state and federal funds in the process.

Yet they helped to collect, write, file, store and proofread this book. Without their support and cooperation, this book would never have been published.

# ACKNOWLEDGEMENTS

Thanks to the *Nevada Appeal* for giving me permission to reprint a few of the articles they ran about me way back when.

INTRODUCTION

I n the 1970s, with social mores changing quickly and
public morals changing slowly, Nevada was tired of being
known as the only state with legal prostitution, and the City
of Reno, located in Washoe County, was tired of living right
next door to Storey County and the famous Mustang Ranch
brothel. Joe Conforte, the owner of Mustang, was a gregarious,
influential, legal power in business and politics. His name
garnered national recognition; his brothel attracted national
curiosity. Where high-profile names and money came into play,
there was Joe Conforte.

Mustang Ranch was a licensed brothel, and Joe Conforte was
a legal businessman. As a local businessman, Conforte wanted
to be involved in his community. Local politicians wanted
campaign contributions, though not necessarily to have their
names linked with Conforte's. Local law enforcement wanted
to take him down. Local newspapers wanted the homegrown
stories with national appeal.

Everybody wanted something. I just wanted to live my life,
run my business (Washoe Realty) and continue serving on the
Reno City Council.

In 1976, Warren Lerude, executive editor of the *Reno Evening
Gazette* and the *Nevada State Journal*, nominated himself and
two of his colleagues for a Pulitzer Prize. The body of work
submitted to the Pulitzer committee dealt with Conforte and
alleged corruption.

The stories centered around a transaction Joe Conforte
had made, purchasing a parcel of land from the Capurro
family and then selling it to the Reno-Sparks Convention
and Visitors Authority to be used as a golf course. The story

broke when the newspapers printed the 48-page grand jury report of the investigation into the land sale. Two-hundred-twenty-nine articles followed the initial article, all bent on exposing corruption, covering the county Organized Crime Unit investigation and the grand jury hearings. The most telling line in Lerude's letter to the Pulitzer committee is: "The editorials tell their own story best." The story told in those editorials is impassioned and entertaining and well-written. But it's not entirely true. In their zeal to topple Joe Conforte, the newspapers sacrificed at least one innocent.

I was linked to Joe Conforte because a REALTOR in my real estate office, Jimmy Smith, handled the land transaction between the Capurro family and Joe Conforte. The subsequent sale from Conforte to the Reno Sparks Visitors Authority was handled by Conforte alone. But my name was listed in the grand jury report. I was questioned by Real Estate Division investigators even though I hadn't handled the transaction myself. I was never indicted for anything. There was nothing illegal about the transaction. But my name was still dragged all the way through the Pulitzer-winning editorials – even after the Nevada Supreme Court ordered my name expunged from the report the grand jury issued tying local politicians to Conforte. I was simply a name that got swept up into the melee, and the supreme court recognized this. Even after the newspapers were given files showing my innocence, the editorials continued to include me. Even after I was harassed by law enforcement, my Real Estate Division files were mysteriously destroyed and my business hurt, the editorials continued.

The publishers weren't after me. But neither was there any evidence that they cared if I was caught up in the intrigue they had created around Joe Conforte and this single land transaction being investigated with an eye toward bringing Conforte down. The story became more important than the truth. Those editorials do tell their stories best – but they tell one side, and it's not the only one.

Here, for the first time and after 30 years, is the other side of the story: my side, the truth. But I'm not going to let just my words alone make my case. This book includes documents, articles and minutes of meetings that map out the terrain of a life interrupted by a story, sacrificed for Pulitzers and shadowed by deception. I'm not here to tell a story; I want to show the truth.

The Pulitzer Prize is awarded for achievement in journalism. Three editorial writers from two Nevada newspapers were awarded the prize even with the faulty reporting and outright malice. It begs the question, what kind of achievement was being awarded here?

I was an innocent bystander in the larger story of Joe Conforte. There's no question of this. My reputation and well-being were sacrificed to the perceived greater good of journalistic entertainment. There are two sides to every story. The following pages finally tell my side.

# WITH MALICE TOWARD ONE:
## A True Story of Prostitution, Politics and a Pulitzer Prize in Nevada

This is Nevada. It's a wide-open state of vast distances and few people, of loners who choose their own way to go and, in the 1970s, the only state with legalized gambling.

It's also the only state – still – to allow individual counties with populations of less than 400,000 decide whether or not to legalize prostitution. In the 1970s, all but six of Nevada's 17 counties had chosen to legalize the profession. The infamous and world-famous bunny ranches outside small towns and big cities in Nevada have attracted attention from every part of the media from *60 Minutes* to *Geraldo Rivera* to the cover of *Rolling Stone*.

In 1967 Joe Conforte took over the Mustang Bridge Ranch brothel in Storey County, Nevada, and renamed it Mustang Ranch (an improvement over his Southern Nevada brothel, Happy Valley). Prostitution is illegal in Washoe County, where Reno is located, but legal in Storey County. Conforte's Mustang Ranch was so close to the county line, just about 10 miles outside Reno city limits, that the brothel's bar was actually in Washoe County. Irritated politicians and lawmen never stopped wanting to bust Conforte for running a legitimate business in what they considered an immoral trade. But by 1971 Conforte was operating Mustang as a legal brothel, and he himself was a legitimate businessman. The stigma of prostitution meant the authorities kept a sharp eye on him, and most of them probably wouldn't have minded finding something to run him in for.

In 1973 Joe Conforte sold a piece of land he'd purchased from a local ranching family (the Capurros) to the Reno-

Sparks Convention Authority. The land would later become the Wildcreek Golf Course. Conforte didn't profit from the sale, receiving less than he'd paid for the acreage sold, but hoped to profit when he sold his adjacent land, which should have increased in value. The way things actually played out, Conforte ended up running into a series of legal problems and eventually lost that piece of land to the IRS.

Conforte's problems would soon become mine, despite the fact that the only thing we had in common was the sale of a parcel of empty land.

On Wednesday, May 15, 1974, two investigators from the Nevada Department of Commerce, Real Estate Division, showed up at my office at Washoe Realty in Reno, Nevada, and began a nightmare that lasted better than 30 years. Investigators Laqua and Baumann wanted to discuss a recent land transaction one of the agents in my office had made. I was a Reno City Councilman at the time and requested the investigators set a date and time to meet, since I was on my way to an appointment when the agents arrived unannounced. I didn't think much of it at the time; I'd been through an investigation once before. In that case, a representative from the Real Estate Division had called and informed me there'd been a mathematical error on a sale. I saw the error when it was pointed out, called the client and reimbursed the amount of the mistake (around $600). I had no reason to be worried about this new investigation – I hadn't done anything wrong.

On Friday, May 17, 1974, I once again found the agents waiting in my office. They said they came to hear my side of a story, a story that involved local politics, Joe Conforte and Mustang Ranch. But they came without a complaint or any evidence of wrongdoing on anyone's part. They didn't produce any complaints against Washoe Realty, they didn't level any charges, and they didn't have any intention of answering questions put to them. Not only that, but they came with a waiver for me to sign: the Miranda warning.

## [Below] Miranda Warning

On Friday, May 17, 1974, my associate James (Jimmy) Smith and I, as a real estate broker and owner of Washoe Realty, met with Nevada Department of Commerce Real Estate Division investigators Laqua and Baumann regarding a legitimate sale of land from the Capurro family to Joe Conforte, owner of the Mustang Ranch brothel. Unlike any investigation I had heard of or participated in, the investigators never produced a complaint from anyone involved in the transaction and never produced the letter directing them to investigate the sale, though they insisted such a letter existed. What they did produce, prior to what they said was nothing more than getting our stories about the sale, was a waiver of rights – a Miranda warning we were asked to sign.

STATE OF NEVADA
DEPARTMENT OF COMMERCE
REAL ESTATE DIVISION
ADMINISTRATIVE OFFICE
CARSON CITY, NEVADA 89701
(702) 882-7809

MIKE O'CALLAGHAN
Governor
MICHAEL L. MELNER
Director
Department of Commerce

R. E. HANSEN
Administrator
Real Estate Division

WAIVER

NAME Clyde Biglieri                    CASE NO. RED VS 51074

You are hereby advised that:

(1) You have the right to remain silent.

(2) Anything you say can and will be used against you in a court of law.

(3) You have the right to talk to a lawyer and have him present with you while you are being questioned.

(4) If you cannot afford to hire a lawyer, one will be appointed to represent you before any questioning, if you wish one.

Do you thoroughly understand each of these rights I have explained to you?_____
(Answer "yes" or "no".)

Having these rights in mind, do you wish to talk to me/us now?_____

Date _____    Time _____    _____
                                   (Signature)

Witness: (1)_____    Title_____
         (2)_____    Title_____

8

The agents wanted to see the file for the Capurro-Conforte transaction, and they wanted to hear my story and that of real estate agent Smith's.

I agreed. I had nothing to hide. The transaction had been fairly standard. But before agreeing to the interview, I asked the investigators if I could see a copy of the complaint against Washoe Realty. Baumann said they didn't have one. I asked if it was customary to investigate a transaction if there was no complaint. Laqua would only say that the administrator of the Real Estate Division had asked them to investigate the sale.

At this point, I asked to see the order to investigate.

The agents feigned confusion.

They stated there was a letter in the file, but they didn't have a copy with them. I asked who the third party was who had requested the investigation. Laqua said he didn't know.

This wasn't normal procedure. Any time a real estate transaction was investigated, it was because a complaint had been made by one of the parties involved, and that complaint was made available for inspection by all of the parties involved.

Rather than comply with the request and open my files with no evidence of a complaint and no cooperation from the investigators, I picked up the phone and called the Real Estate Division in Carson City, Nevada's capital, and asked to speak with the administrator. The administrator was out of town, though his secretary offered to look in the file. A few minutes later she returned to the phone and said she couldn't locate the letter authorizing the investigation. She referred me to Bob Edmondson at the Attorney General's office.

When I reached Edmondson, I was told there was a letter but that the administrator, who was out of town and out of touch, unable to be contacted, had the letter with him. He said the administrator had the right to investigate anything he wanted to.

I didn't argue. I had never argued with the Real Estate Division investigators. I simply wanted to know why the transaction was being investigated and who had signed the letter on file. Edmondson refused to tell me and refused to divulge the contents of the letter.

I asked him if he received 25 complaints to investigate would he just do so? Edmondson said yes. I said I thought that was a waste of the taxpayers' money.

I asked Edmondson again why he was checking out the Capurro-Conforte sale, and Edmondson replied, "Haven't you been reading the newspaper?" I had, but that didn't explain anything.

When I asked again why the commission was investigating the sale, the answer was growing familiar: they could investigate anything they wanted to. I again agreed they had the right but that I still wanted to see the letter authorizing the investigation of Washoe Realty.

The phone conversation with Edmondson ended shortly thereafter.

## "HAVEN'T YOU BEEN READING THE NEWSPAPER?"

In the 1970s, Reno had two daily newspapers, the *Nevada State Journal* and the *Reno Evening Gazette*, both owned by Speidel. The comment regarding whether I was up-to-date with the recent news pertained to news coverage of the ongoing investigation of the land sale between Conforte and the Convention Authority. There had been articles about the sale, but that was hardly unusual – everything Conforte did was under scrutiny. That happened to businessmen whose business was prostitution, legal or otherwise.

Once the discussion with Edmondson about the complaint – or lack thereof – had ended, Investigator Laqua asked me if they could proceed with the interview. Since I'd set the morning aside to meet with the investigators and tell them my story, I agreed. That was when the investigators produced the Miranda waiver and asked me to sign.

The Miranda warning is traditionally read by police when they arrest suspects, ever since Miranda v. Arizona 384 US 436 (1966.) By signing, I would acknowledge my right to remain silent, that anything I said could be used against me if the case – if there were a case – went to trial, and that I had the right to an attorney, something I didn't need since I hadn't done anything wrong.

I refused to sign. In the past, only one complaint had ever been filed against Washoe Realty and at that time when I asked, I had been allowed to see the complaint. I'd cooperated 100 percent, and I'd never been asked to sign a Miranda warning. Being asked to sign a waiver now felt like a threat.

"If you won't sign, there's no reason for us to stay," Laqua said. He put the waiver in his briefcase and walked across the building to Smith's office. Smith was the real estate agent who had actually handled the Capurro-Conforte transaction.

Smith also felt something about the investigators' visit was odd. He had to ask four times to see the waiver so he could decide whether or not to sign it, and neither investigator was disposed to let him see it. When Smith did finally read the waiver, he also refused to sign.

Being asked to sign a Miranda waiver was just too close to being accused of something.

Laqua asked if either of us would give him a statement. I said we'd give the investigators all the time they wanted, but we weren't offering up the file without being able to see a complaint, and we weren't signing the waiver. Laqua asked for a signed, written statement, and I again refused.

Laqua demanded to know why we wouldn't sign. I said I was afraid the waiver might get lost or news about it end up printed in the newspaper. My concerns ended up looking like a premonition.

Laqua took offense, bristled at what he interpreted as an accusation of his intention to leak the information, and called Edmondson in Carson City about the waiver. Edmondson must have urged Laqua to simply get the story as Smith and I had originally indicated we would give it since the investigators then asked for the story even without the signed waiver.

However, we were no longer willing. The guarded behavior of the two investigators and their refusal to explain anything about the alleged complaint had put both of us on edge. I made a counter-offer: Smith and I would accompany Laqua and Baumann to the Washoe County Sheriff's Office and sign a release giving the investigators permission to read the Sheriff's Office file. I assumed there was a file – after all, the Sheriff's

Office was investigating the Conforte-Convention Authority land transaction.

"I'll give you whatever you need," I told them, meaning I'd tell them what I knew. "I just won't sign the Miranda warning waiver."

The investigators relented. They put their briefcases back down and sat in my office and listened to my story, and later that morning, they listened to Smith's story.

The two agents left shortly before lunch, and at the time, though I was concerned and on the defensive, I had no way of anticipating the hell that was about to break loose in my life.

Today Wildcreek Golf Course is located on Sullivan Lane, in Sparks, Nevada, Reno's next-door neighbor. But in 1974 the course was still just the dream of the Reno-Sparks Convention Authority. The Convention Authority was, at that time, an administrative body made up of five representative members, two from the City of Reno, one from the City of Sparks and two from Washoe County. It was responsible for promoting tourism in Northern Nevada.

At the time, I was a City of Reno Councilman, Ward 4. My real estate office had not handled the transaction that sold the land to the Convention Authority – Conforte had sold the land himself – but I wanted to be certain I didn't do anything unethical by voting on the hotel room tax increase proposed to pay for the golf course that would be built on the land sold to the Convention Authority. So I abstained from the first vote held in March 1974 and didn't vote until the issue came up again in August 1974 (by which time well over a year had passed since Smith handled the sale of the Capurro land to Conforte), at which point I voted in favor of the increase in order to break a tie (I later received an opinion from the ethics commission to validate that this was not an unethical decision with the amount of time that had passed).

My abstention was a matter of common sense: I wasn't concerned that my office had been part of the land transaction, because the transaction had occurred 14 months earlier (and, as it turned out, the ethics commission advised that only 12 months needed to pass before I voted); I was concerned because I owned an interest in a motel located in Reno. Motel owners collect the room tax in Nevada and are responsible for disbursing it to the taxing authorities and keeping the books. In return, they keep 2 percent of what they collect.

I abstained. Bob Rusk (Robert Rusk, Washoe County Commissioner) also abstained, but Sam Dibitonto (Mayor, City of Reno) voted, and both of them also owned motels in Reno.

So I voted, and my vote was a tie-breaker. The motion to increase the sales tax on hotel and motel rooms in order to pay for the construction of Wildcreek Golf Course passed.

## [Pages 17-24] Reno City Council Meeting Minutes

Minutes from Reno City Council meetings held August 12, 1974, and March 10, 1975. Both sets of minutes reference the vote on the proposed increase in motel room taxes by $.01 by the Convention Authority.

*PAGE #14*
*Room TAX*

RENO CITY COUNCIL
BRIEF OF MINUTES
(Official Minutes in City Clerk's Office)
AUGUST 12, 1974

TAPE ONE-SIDE ONE

610 - 684

A regular meeting of the Reno City Council was called to order at 9:00 a.m. Monday, August 12, 1974 in the Council Chambers of the City Hall.

PRESENT:       Councilmen Lauri, Lewis, Sorensen, Bogart, Biglieri, Menicucci, Dibitonto
ALSO PRESENT:  City Manager Latimore, City Attorney Van Wagoner, Chief Deputy City Clerk Mandagaran

### APPROVAL OF MINUTES

June 24; July 8, 1974

It was moved by Councilman Biglieri, seconded by Councilman Menicucci the minutes of the Council meetings of June 24 and July 8, 1974 be approved as submitted. Motion carried.

### APPROVAL REGULAR CURRENT BILLS

It was moved by Councilman Bogart, seconded by Councilman Lauri we approve payment of general fund regular warrants #00200 thru #00277, #00278 thru 00398 and #00399 thru #00500 with the exception of warrant #00327.

The motion was carried by the following roll call vote:
AYES:    Councilmen Bogart, Lauri, Lewis, Sorensen, Biglieri, Menicucci Dibitonto

******

Approval of Warrant #35- Board of Regents

It was moved by Councilman Lauri, seconded by Councilman Bogart we approve payment of Warrant #35, in the amount of $900.00 to Board of Regents which was withheld from the last regular Council meeting approval of warrants.

The  motion was carried by the following roll call vote:
AYES:    Councilmen Lauri, Bogart, Lewis, Sorensen, Biglieri, Dibitonto
NAYS:    Councilman Menicucci

### SPECIAL BILLS AND CLAIMS

Final Payment, Contract #212

It was moved by Councilman Menicucci, seconded by Councilman Bogart we approve final payment, Contract #212, modifications South Keystone and California Avenue, Helms Construction in the amount of $10,649.77.

The motion was carried by the following roll call vote:
AYES:    Councilman Menicucci, Bogart, Lauri, Lewis, Sorensen, Biglieri Dibitonto

******

Final Payment, Contract #247

It was moved by Councilman Menicucci, seconded by Councilman Biglieri we app final payment, Contract #247, 1973 Street Improvement Program, Helms Construction Company in the amount of $45,921.48.

The motion was carried by the following roll call vote:
AYES:    Councilmen Menicucci, Biglieri, Lauri, Lewis, Sorensen, Bogart Dibitonto

-1-

8/12/74

Attorney Sidney Robinson appeared before the Council to review in depth the report of Consulting Engineer Milton Sharp as to the removal of debris and rubble at 133 North Virginia Street. Mr. Robinson advised that August 9, 1974 a meeting of the property owners was held with Milton Sharp, Mr. Brunzell and the Building Inspector. In reviewing the report from Milton Sharp, it was noted by Mr. Robinson that his clients are prepared to do anything the City would request if the Council wishes it down under the hazardous conditions as outlined.

The Chief Building Inspector appeared before the Council to advise that he concurs with the recommendations set out by Milton Sharp but even if this corrective work is done at 133 N. Virginia Street there still remains the problem with the Wonder Building and the repair to this wall was temporary in nature. Councilman Bogart noted that the City should proceed immediately to take concrete action in this matter and that the City should have a hold harmless agreement. The Chief Building Inspector concurred that steps should be taken to correct the entire problem at 133 N. Virginia and 135 North Virginia Fire Marshall Upson appeared before the Council to review his recent inspection of the 133 North Virginia Street site.

It was moved by Councilman Bogart, seconded by Councilman Lewis the conditions that now exist at 133 North Virginia Street shall be entirely removed under the supervision of Sharp, Krater and Associates and the Building Department and that there shall be a hold harmless agreement to the city, holding the city harmless.

Under discussion, Mr. Robinson questioned why a hold harmless agreement should be required since he could not see where the City had any liability in this matter.

Councilman Sorensen noted that the Wonder Building should be torn down before clean up work is started at 133 North Virginia Street.

The motion was carried by the following roll call vote:
AYES:    Councilmen Bogart, Lewis, Lauri, Biglieri, Menicucci, Dibitonto
NAYS:    Councilman Sorensen

625 - 734        SPECIAL REQUESTS CON'T

Re-review of request of Reno Convention Authority for Room Tax Increase

For the benefit of those present the Mayor re-reviewed the request of the Reno Convention Authority for an increase in room tax, advising that those present would be given the opportunity to present their views.

Nick Lusich, President of the Chamber of Commerce appeared before the Council in favor of the increase advising that the Chamber needs additional funds for the promotion of tourism for this area, that funds are needed to proceed with the proposed golf course, and that most every city on the west coast has a 6% room tax.

Jud Allen appeared before the Council speaking on behalf of the Chamber of Commerce in favor of the increase and advising that too much emphasis has been put on how these funds will be spent, that the funds in the past have been well spent, and that in comparing Reno with Las Vegas, it is clear that Reno must get in and correct some of our problems.

County Commissioner Gerry Grow appeared before the Council in favor of the increase advising that these funds could be used to make the area more attractive for tourism and that, after all, is what we are interested in.

Attorney Clinton Wooster representing the Nevada State Motel Association appeared before the Council. He advised that there are 197 motels in this area opposed to the increase and that most of the City's hotels also opposed it.

-14-

Mr. Wooster advised that if the present proposed priorities can be financed with existing revenue and that if there is an increase in the room tax and these priorities are funded from that source of revenue, any remaining funds will be allocated to the Chamber of Commerce for their use; Mr. Wooster noted that an increase in room tax was not necessary for that purpose.

In continuing, Mr. Wooster pointed out that new hotels under construction will bring in the same amount of revenue as an increase to the room tax will bring in and that the Convention Authority at this time had no projects before it that could justify this increase. Councilman Bogart advised that the Convention Authority had been asked to reveal all proposed projects and these amounted to approximately $32,000,000.

Chuck Munson on behalf of Harrah's Club appeared before the Council to advise they have not changed their position, that they are opposed and there is no real need for the increase, nor any real plans for the use of the money. In reply to Councilman Lewis, Mr. Munson gave a brief outline of the promotional and advertising plans carried on by Harrah's Club; Mr. Munson advised he did not have actual figures at his command but would furnish them if the Council wished. Councilman Biglieri pointed out that Harrahs and the Sparks Nugget must spend more than a million dollars a year to bring tourists to this area.

Pat Jordan, President of the Motel-Hotel Association appeared before the Council advising that under our present economics, this increase in room tax can not be justified. A lady in the audience appeared, advising that she owns seven motels, and her income has been down the last year.

There appeared to be no others present who wished to speak in this matter.

734 - 808

There followed a general discussion by Councilmen Lewis and Lauri on the proposed golf course with Mr. Grow advising that no funds have been spent on this land as yet, but if the land is not developed into a golf course the seller has the option to buy the land back at the purchase price. In reply to Councilman Lauri who asked who would oversee the construction of the golf course and the maintenance, Mr. Grow advised there would be an Advisory Committee for this project. Mr. Grow also advised Councilman Lauri that the Convention Authority did not wish to go into debt by going to bond. In reply to Councilman Lewis, Mr. Grow outlined the criteria that had been used in selecting priorities. Councilman Lauri questioned if it was proper to impose a tax for a golf course when it was not known who would build it or maintain it. Mr. Grow pointed out that when the increase in room tax had first been requested, the priorities had not been established.

It was moved by Councilman Bogart, seconded by Councilman Menicucci that the room tax be increased from 5% to 6%.

Under discussion, Councilman Biglieri reiterated remarks made a previous meetings as to why he would abstain from voting in this matter, but advising that were he not abstaining he would vote for the increase.

Councilman Lauri advised that it is a matter of recklessness to plan projects without sufficient funds and it was never the purpose in increasing the room tax to provide money for the Chamber of Commerce and that no other tax would be increased for this purpose. Councilman Lauri advised he would vote against the motion.

Councilman Menicucci advised that he seconded the motion and he feels we should reassess ourselves, that we are a tourist oriented city and we should think of our economy first.

-15-

8/12/74

Councilman Lewis noted that we should think about the greatest good for the community and the tourists do have the advantage of many of the services offered them by the City; however, this would be an autonomous board and there should be some control from the community but this is missing.

The following roll call vote resulted in no action on the motion:
AYES:       Councilmen Bogart, Menicucci, Lewis
NAYS:       Councilmen Lauri, Sorensen, Dibitonto
ABSTAIN:    Councilman Biglieri

Councilman Biglieri advised that he was going to change his abstention and vote in this matter. Councilman Lauri questioned if Councilman Biglieri could change his vote after having announced he would abstain. Councilman Menicucci noted, that by our own rules of this Council, this is up to the individual. Councilman Lauri pointed out that the roll call have been complete and when completed one can not change his vote and if there is to be a new vote, the entire matter must be reconsidered.

It was  moved by Councilman Bogart, seconded by Councilman Menicucci we reconsider the previous Council action concerning the increase in room tax. Motion carried.

It was moved by Councilman Bogart, seconded by Councilman Menicucci we approve the request to increase the room tax from 5% to 6%.

The motion was carried by the following roll call vote:
AYES:       Councilmen Bogart, Menicucci, Lewis, Biglieri
NAYS:       Councilmen Lauri, Sorensen, Dibitonto

809 - 844       REPORTS OF MAYOR, CITY MANAGER & COMMITTEES CON'T

Letter from University-17.1 Acres to be developed Through Recreational Progra

It was moved by Councilman Menicucci, seconded by Councilman Sorensen we acknowledge receipt of the letter, as read in full by the Mayor, from the University of Nevada regarding 17.1 acres to be developed by the College of Agriculture through the recreation program, and that the University of Nevada be commended for this action on their part. Motion carried.

******

Notice from Public Service Commission Dismissing Application-Cancelling Heari

It was moved by Councilman Sorensen, seconded by Councilman Bogart we acknowledge receipt of notice from Public Service Commission of Order dismissing Application and cancelling hearing in the request of Sierra Pacific Power to revise certain tariffs applicable to its electric department, hearing to have been held August 9, 1974 at 2:00 p.m. Holiday Inn, S. Virginia Street. Motion carried.

******

Before PSC Power Company application to increase Certain Gas Dept. Rates

It was moved by Councilman Bogart, seconded by Councilman Lewis we acknowledge notice of Application before Public Service Commission of Sierra Pacific Power to increase certain of its rate schedules applicable to its gas department. Motion carried.
******

Before PSC Power Company Application to Increase Certain Electric Dept. Rates

It was moved by Councilman Sorensen, seconded by Councilman Bogart we acknowledge notice of  Application before Public Service Commission of Sierra Pacific Power to increase certain of its rate schedules applicable to its electric department. Motion carried.
******

Before PSC Power Company Application to Increase Certain Water Dept. Rates

It was moved by Councilman Menicucci, seconded by Councilman Sorensen we
-16-                                                          8/12/74

18

RENO
CITY
COUNCIL
MEETING
ABOUT
3-10-7?

SPECIAL REQUESTS CON'T

### Request of City Clerk-Gypsum Anti Trust Cases

It was moved by Councilman Lauri, seconded by Councilman Bogart we approve the request of the City Clerk to authorize him to file claims on behalf of the city in the Gypsum Anti-Trust cases. Motion carried.

\*\*\*\*\*\*

758 - 840

### Request of Convention Authority - .01¢ Increase in Room Tax

The request of the Reno-Sparks Convention Authority for a .01¢ increase in the room tax was presented for discussion.

Mr. Charles Udey, 1800 Sullivan Lane, a retired plumber, appeared before the Council to read a prepared statement in regard to his opposition to the proposed increase.

Jim Weaver, Chamber of Commerce appeared before the Council on behalf of the Chamber President, Mr. Lucini and advising they are in favor of the increase.

Roy Powers appeared before the Council to advise at the request of the Chamber of Commerce Convention Authority he had made several visits within the State and to California and found the room tax to be 6% and up and that the cities he had visited suffered no hardship by an increase in room tax. It was also noted that the Chamber of Commerce recommended that an Advisory Committee be appointed for the disbursement of these excess monies.

Sue Griswold, Nevada Art Gallery appeared to advise they are in favor of the increase to support a cultural center.

Will Jurgens of the Chamber of Commerce appeared to advise he would be in favor of the increase, and that an increase in room tax would have no adverse effect on booking conventions.

Don Carano appeared before the Council in favor of the increase tax and advising that he spoke for the Holiday Hotel, El Dorado Hotel, and Pioneer Inn.

Donna Walsh, Nevada Art Gallery appeared in favor of the increase to support a cultural center.

Charles Gladney, Sierra Arts Foundation appeared before the Council in favor of the increase in tax and to speak at great length on a proposed cultural center which is reported to be number three on the priority list for expenditure of the excess funds. Another representative of the Nevada Art Gallery appeared to advise she was in favor of the increase in order to suppor the proposed cultural center.

James Vernon, Sparks Councilman and Chairman of the Convention Authority appeared before the Council to speak at great length on the benefits that would be derived from an increase in the room tax. Mr. Vernon advised the Council that the original room tax had been used to construct the present facilities. Proposed projects from excess funds would be used to add a dining room to the present coliseum, a golf course in Sparks, and the proposed cultural center.

### TAPE ONE-SIDE TWO

000 - 125

In answer to Councilman Lauri, Mr. Vernon advised that the estimated cost of the dining facility is $1.2 million, and that to date only the three prioritie as outlined has been planned for the excess money.

-15-

Councilman Bogart noted that an Advisory Board had made recommendations on the priority system for consideration by the Convention Authority.

Jerry Grow, County Commissioner serving on the Convention Authority appeared before the Council advising that NRS 244.640 legally constitutes the Convention Authority, that the gross tax for 1972-73 would have generated approximately $300,000 in additional funds if the tax had been increased.

Councilman Lewis asked what the operating costs had amounted to during the last year paid from the room tax. Mayor Dibitonto advised that he had this break down and presented a copy of this to Councilman Lewis. The Mayor also advised that he had a break down of all taxes received since the inception of the room tax.

In continuing, Mr. Grow advised that the room tax is no deterent to tourism, that it will benefit the local businessman and everyone involved, but if we do not try for an increase we would be guilty of sitting still and going backwards.

Mayor Dibitonto asked if the proposed increase has anything to do with the bonding capacity of the Convention Authority. Mr. Grow advised that this had not been fully explored but that he would prefer to go on short time financing paying cash as they go. Mr. Grow also noted they could have gone to bond before this time and accomplished their priorities; also, the original intent of the tax monies had been for bettering fair and recreation facilities the first consideration of the revenue is to retire the bonds.

Mr. Udey appeared briefly again, advising he had come to this meeting to hear the vote on the room tax, not all this talk about the revenue that had been generated, or that could be generated.

James Lillard, Sparks Mayor appeared before the Council in favor of the increase and advising that there has been too much emphasis on how the excess money will be spent, rather than stressing the need for the increase. It was noted that there have been requests for local improvements that would require fifty to sixty million dollars and this increase in room tax would help provide some of these needed improvements.

## 125 - 245

John Hardy, 230 Caliente Street appeared before the Council advising that he is opposed to the increase in tax because he has to collect it, that the motels and hotels were being pressured into this increase, and if additional funds are needed other areas should be taxed, such as the real estate brokers or insurance businesses.

Clinton Wooster, Attorney representing the Nevada State Motel Association appeared before the Council to present a petition sponsored by the Motel Association members opposed to the increase. Mr. Wooster read into the record the reasons set out in the petition of opposition. It was noted that the Convention Authority now has ample funds to build the dining facility and that their second and third priority are not concrete at this time. It was also pointed out by Mr. Wooster that under the 5% bonding capacity the Convention Authority now has the capacity to fund the golf course and the cultural center. Additionally, Mr. Wooster pointed out that there are some 2,000 new hotel rooms presently under construction, all of which will add to the room tax.

Attorney William Raggio appeared before the Council on behalf of the Nevada State Motel Association, repeating and concurring in remarks presented by Clinton Wooster. Mr. Raggio advised that the increase would be a breech of faith with the spirit of the law, that the tax was to retire the bond debt, and it is incumbent on elected officials to know the law and to apply responsibility in dealing with it and that at this point in time there was no need for the Convention Authority to increase this tax unless the need had been adequately demonstrated, which it had not.

ROOM TAX

Pat Jordan, Nevada State Motel Association, President, appeared before the
Council opposing the increase and advising with the current energy crisis
this is not the time to think of added taxes; also, the Convention Authority
could get a short time loan for construction of their priority projects.

245 - 354

Chuck Munson from Harrah's Club appeared before the Council advising that
Harrah's has been opposed to the increase since it had first been proposed.
Additionally, Mr. Munson advised that though the Chamber of Commerce may be
in favor of this increase, many, many Chamber of Commerce members were opposed
and the Chamber did not speak for their entire membership.

Jerry Higgins of the Sparks Nugget appeared before the Council to advise
that the Nugget has not taken a position against the proposed golf course
but they have taken the position opposing the increase in room tax and that
the priorities can be accomplished under the present five million dollar
bonding capacity.

Councilman Lewis questioned if the Convention Authority would be interested
in bonding for the three priorities, and when the time came that there was
a more intense need for additional tax the matter could be reconsidered.
Mr. Grow advised that the Convention Authority could go to bond but everytime
this is done all the property in the County has to be put up for security
and revenues pledged for years which would mean that money would not be
available for new needs. Mr. Grow also advised that at the meeting of the
hotel and motel owners, only ten persons appeared in opposition; therefore,
he did not feel that the petition that had been presented to be valid.
As to fiscal responsibility, Mr. Grow advised that the State law stipulates
how this money can be spent.

Councilman Lauri noted that if the bonding capacity is here and with the
increment increase in room tax revenues, the problem of additional money
would appear to be solved.

Councilman Biglieri advised the Council that the County does not have a
conflict of interest law, while the City just recently passed one and that
since he owns an interest in a motel he was going to abstain from voting
on this issue. Councilman Biglieri also noted that the Convention Authority
has the bonding capacity, the land in the County is a good buy, but the County
is not providing any recreation or park facilities for the people while Reno
and Sparks have been providing this.

Douglas Gray, motel operator appeared before the Council opposed to the tax
increase, advising that he has given the Fair and Recreation Board over the
years more than $75,000 and has never had the opportunity to say anything as
to how these funds would be used. He also noted that the Chamber of Commerce
appears to be in the hotel,motel reservation business and this is not right.

Mr. Raggio appeared to rebut the statement made by Mr. Grow as to their paying
cash for their projects, advising that this would not be advantageous and
since the bonding capacity is avilable it should be used.

Councilman Lauri asked Mr. Vernon if the City of Reno defeated this increase
in room tax would they then go to the bonding issue. Mr. Vernon advised that
since he is only one member of the Convention Authority he could not answer
this question. Councilman Menicucci advised that it would appear we are
caught in a cross fire of priorities and this has become a very emotional
issue.

354 - 403

It was moved by Councilman Bogart, seconded by Councilman Sorensen we go on
record as being in favor of the .01¢ increase in room tax.

Under discussion, the Mayor advised that he had been elected to his office
because he could walk and talk and he was going to vote against the motion.

The motion resulted in a tie vote by the following roll call vote:
AYES:       Councilmen Bogart, Sorensen, Menicucci
NAYS:       Councilmen Lauri, Lewis, Dibitonto
ABSTAIN:    Councilman Biglieri

-17-

Councilman Lewis advised that she voted against the motion because of lack of information. Councilman Menicucci advised that he had never seen a report on Convention Authority meetings. Councilman Biglieri advised that he had abstained because of conflict of interest.

The City Attorney advised that there was no action on the vote and for the benefit of the Council read portions of the conflict of interest law, noting that if one of the Council abstains on a vote he must make a disclosure of his reason. Councilman Biglieri advised that we did not pass a disclosure law but passed a conflict of interest. Councilman Biglieri noted that since now information had come before the Council today, and since we had a no vote this matter could be rescheduled and perhaps at that time if he felt that he could vote he would do so.

In a general discussion, Mr. Grow advised the Council that there is an option on the golf course land until April 6, 1974. The Mayor advised that though this may be true they can still go to a bonding issue for this land.

Mr. Vernon invited the Council to the next meeting of the Convention Authority March 28, 1974 at 1:00 p.m. in the hope that more information could be furnished for the Reno City Council. Councilman Lauri suggested that the Convention Authority go for the bond issue and ask for the tax increase at a later date. Councilman Lauri also noted that Reno generates 70 to 80% of the tax money in this area and the other entities that would approve this tax increase are in the minority.

No further action at todays meeting.

404 - 428                    AIRPORT IMPROVEMENTS

## March 21, 1974 Airports Advisory Commission Meeting

Councilman Biglieri reported on the March 21, 1974 Airports Advisory Commission meeting which resulted in the following action by the Council.

## Renewal Agreement-1974 National Air Races

It was moved by Councilman Biglieri, seconded by Councilman Sorensen we approve the renewal agreement for the use of Reno/Stead for the 1974 National Championship Air Races and the Mayor be authorized to sign. Motion carried.

\*\*\*\*\*\*\*

## Fourth Rent-a-Car Agency at Airport

It was moved by Councilman Biglieri, seconded by Councilman Lauri we approve a fourth rent-a-car agency at Reno International Airport with interested agencies to submit proposals to the Airports Advisory Commission for review and recommendation to the City Council. Motion carried.

\*\*\*\*\*\*

## Autocross Events at Reno/Stead Airport

It was moved by Councilman Biglieri, seconded by Councilman Sorensen we approve the renewal of permit agreement, and authorize the Mayor to sign, Sports Car Club of America, Reno Region and/or Sierra Nevada Region of Porsche Car Club of America for auto cross events at Reno/Stead Airport on the dates set forth in Exhibit C of the renewal agreement. Motion carried.

\*\*\*\*\*\*

## Janitorial Work at Airport

The Mayor advised that more personnel is needed for the janitorial work at the airport and in view of the salaries involved and the cost of equipment, it has been suggested that this janitorial work be put out on a contract.

-18-

Everything should have been fine. I could ethically vote on the issue, and the sale of the Capurro land to Conforte was on the up-and-up. Even if Conforte's role as a brothel owner was frowned on in some sectors, he was still a legitimate business owner.

However, everything wasn't fine. Because Conforte was involved, a grand jury was convened to look into the sale of the land, and two years after the sale – two years after Investigators Laqua and Baumann had showed up in my office – the grand jury released a report. The report accused me of a conflict of interest. This accusation was false.

A series of letters between me and Angus W. McLeod of the Nevada Department of Commerce, Real Estate Division, in late 1975 and early 1976, and an advisory opinion from the State of Nevada Ethics Commission dated February 21, 1976, show that the Ethics Commission found no conflict of interest in my voting on the room tax increase.

**[Below] Letter from me to State of Nevada Ethics Commission**
In his letter, dated January 10, 1976, I requested an opinion on my use of conflict-of-interest guidelines regarding
the Reno City Council room tax vote.

# Washoe Realty

"Real Estate... Sold The Right Way"

1100 KIETZKE LANE • P.O. BOX 911 • RENO, NEVADA 89502 • TELEPHONE (702) 786-6932

Reno, Nevada
January 10, 1976

State of Nevada Ethics Commission

Dear Sirs:

I would appreciate it if you could consider this letter
as a request of your commission to render an opinion
for my personal use as a guideline in various areas
concerning the Conflict of Interest Law # A.B. 610. I
am the owner of Washoe Realty in Reno, and also a
duly elected City Councilman of The City of Reno.

I have read and hopefully understand the intent and content
of this law as passed by the last legislature, but would
certainly appreciate a definite opinion from your body,
if this is practical and within the jurisdiction of the
commission.

The question, and I must state that it is a hypothetical
case, would be as follows: Realtor Clyde Biglieri, or
some Realtor associated with my office and working under
my brokers license at Washoe Realty, acting as an agent,
sells a piece of real estate to a buyer. The transaction
closes in normal fashion, Washoe Realty is paid the full
commission due and does not retain any interest, either
from the buyer or seller, Either direct or indirect.
The question then would be: if three months, three years
or any indefinite time after the closing of the escrow,
the buyer comes before the Reno City Council for some
type of requested change involving this particular piece
of property, requiring a vote of the city council, would
I, in any way, have a conflict of interest in voting
either for or against the question

I look forward to hearing from you on this request for an
opinion and once again I would like to stress that your
answer to this question is for my own guidance in trying
to do the very best job I am capable of doing for the
citizens of Reno.

Sincerely,

*Clyd E Biglieri*

Clyde E. Biglieri

24

**[Pages 27-28] Letter / advisory opinion 76-4 from State of Nevada Ethics Commission**
On February 21, 1976, Fr. Larry Dunphy, chairman, State of Nevada Ethics Commission, sent me the response to my question about my use of ethics guidelines in the room tax increase. The opinion indicated that I took the appropriate action by making known my involvement in the land transaction, in the amount of time that had passed, and that I abstained from the vote until the City Council was deadlocked and couldn't move forward on the issue without my vote.

(H.)

State Of Nevada
ETHICS COMMISSION
P.O. Box 7339
Las Vegas, Nv. 89101
Februray 21, 1976

Re: ADVISORY OPINION NO. 76-4

Clyde E. Biglieri
Washoe Realty
1100 Kietzke Lane
P.O. Box 911
Reno, Nv. 89502

Dear Mr. Biglieri:

You have asked us whehter you would have a conflict of interest in voting as a member of the City Council for some change on a piece of property which had been sold by yourself or another agent acting under your broker's license and such sale having been completed in normal fashion, with the full commission having been paid and no interest either direct or indirect being retained? You ask whether three months, three years, or an indefinite period of time makes any difference?

RESPONSE: In the Nevada Ethics in Government Law, some very clear and definite guidelines on this are set out. That section of the Nevada Ethics in Government Law, entitled: "Prohibitions" (NRS 281.700) in subsections 1. & 2(c) set out very clearly that you could not take action, i.e., vote, nor could you attempt to influence such an action for a period of 12 months after the completion of the transaction and the last of your fees had actually been received; so that if the matter of the transaction was finally closed and the last of your fees for the transaction received on March 1rst, 1976, you would have to refrain from voting on attempting to influence any decision of the City Council regarding a change of such property until March 2, 1977. This conclusion is arrived at by reading NRS 281.700 1. & 2(c) which say:

1. A public officer shall not participate in, or in any way attempt to influence, governmental action or decisions relating to any matter within the responsibilities of his public agency in which he knows or has reason to believe he has an economic interest.
2. A public officer has an economic interest in a matter if the action or decision will have a material economic effect on:
. . . .

(c) Any general source of income, delinquent unsecured loans, or gifts aggregating $250 or more in value

received or pormised to the public officer within 12·
months prior to the time when the action is taken or the
decision made; or"

Hence, it is very clear that for 12 months after receiving income
of $250 or more for a person or business, etc. that you cannot
either take action upon nor attempt to influence any matter that
might come before the City Council regarding that person, business,
or whatever.

In the presumably rare event that the City Council could
not take action without your participation, subsection 3 of NRS
281.700 provides that you could take action, if (you):

TIE
1078

(1) Specifically discloses as a matter of official public
record the existence of any economic interest described in
subsection 2;
(2) Describes with particularity the nature of the
interest before he acts or decides or participates in
any action or decision; and
(3) In no way attempts to influence any other public
officer with respect to the matter."

Again, the Commission points out that this special provision for
taking action despite the conflict of interest applies only to
the case (presumably rare) in which the City Council could not
legally act if you did not participate.

The Commission would point out also that beyond the
12 month prohibition on action and influencing, that, prudence
would dictate that you declare you business relationship at the
time of the action so that it is not brought out later on
and embarassing questions and investigations raised by third parties
later on.

Sincerely,

ETHICS COMMISSION
Fr. Larry Dunphy, Chairman.

[Pages 29-31] Advisory Opinion 77-1 from State of Nevada Ethics Commission to me
Advisory opinion, dated November 9, 1977, to me. The Ethics Commission again found that I acted within ethical guidelines with regard to my August 1974 vote on the room-tax increase pursuant to Reno-Sparks Convention Authority's purchase of the Conforte land to build the Wildcreek Golf Course.

STATE OF NEVADA
ETHICS COMMISSION

November 9, 1977

Honorable Clyde E. Biglieri
P. O. Box 911
Reno, Nevada  89502

Advisory Opinion 77-1

Dear Mr. Biglieri:

You requested the advice of the Legislative Ethics Commission concerning the propriety of your future ethical conduct as a public officer of the City of Reno under the following hypothetical fact situation.

## FACTS

As a licensed real estate broker, you or a realtor acting under your license as an agent, sell a piece of real estate to a buyer. The transaction closes in a normal fashion and your firm is paid the full commission due and does not retain any interest, direct or indirect, from either the buyer or seller in the transaction. Subsequently, the buyer comes before the Reno City Council, of which you are a member, seeking some action of the Council for his benefit.

## QUESTION

If the buyer brings this matter before the City Council three months, three years or at any indefinite date after the closing of escrow in the above-mentioned transaction, would you have a conflict of interest in voting either for or against the question raised by the buyer?

## ANALYSIS

NRS 281.481(1) of the Code of Ethical Standards promulgated in the Nevada Ethics In Government Law provides

27

Honorable Clyde E. Biglieri
November 9, 1977
Page Two

that no public officer may accept any emolument or economic
opportunity which would tend improperly to influence a
reasonable person from a faithful and impartial discharge of
his public duties. NRS 281.481(2) of the Code of Ethical
Standards provides that no public officer may use his position
in government to secure unwarranted privileges or advantages
for himself or his business entity.

        Under the fact situation presented to the Commission,
there would not appear to be any violation of NRS 281.481(1),
since the transaction would be completed and you would
retain no interest in the matter at the time the buyer
subsequently brings his problem to the City Council for
resolution. Assuming that no interest is retained by you in
the transaction, either monetary or equitable, at the time
of your vote, you could not receive any emolument or economic
opportunity which would improperly influence your vote.
Your compensation for the transaction would already have
been paid.

        However, it would be important that no representa-
tion or encouragement would previously be made by you or
your agents to the buyer at the time of the transaction that
the buyer could expect a favorable vote by the City Council
when his problem subsequently came before the Council. If
such a representation was made, and even if the transaction
was completed before the buyer's matter came before the
Council, you, as a public officer, would be in violation of
NRS 281.481(2). This would be because you would have used
your official position to obtain an advantage for your
business which may not otherwise have gone to your firm.

## CONCLUSION

        Assuming that a real estate broker or his agents
have not retained any equitable or monetary interest in a
real estate transaction and that the transaction is closed
and ended, and further assuming that no representation was
made to the buyer by the broker or his agents that the buyer
may expect favorable action by the City Council, of which
the broker is a member, on a problem to be subsequently
brought before the City Council by the buyer, it is the
opinion of the Legislative Ethics Commission that the broker,

Honorable Clyde E. Biglieri
November 9, 1977
Page Three

as a member of the City Council, would not be involved in a
conflict of interest in voting on the matter.  It is the
opinion of the Legislative Ethics Commission that this would
be the case regardless of whether the matter came before the
City Council three months, three years or any indefinite date
after the close of the real estate transaction.

Opinions of the Legislative Ethics Commission are
confidential unless released by the requesting party or unless
the public officer or employee involved acts in contravention
of the opinion, in which case the Commission may disclose the
content of the opinion.  NRS 281.511.

Sincerely,

THE LEGISLATIVE ETHICS COMMISSION

By _____
Chairman

MC/ema

**[Below] Grand Jury Report**
Tuesday, March 16, 1976, the *Nevada State Journal* (then owned by Reno Newspapers, Inc.) printed the grand jury report investigating the Capurro-Conforte-RSCVA land transaction in its entirety, despite the fact that several of the individuals mentioned in the report were never indicted for any kind of criminal activity. My life changed when the grand jury report was filed and the 229 newspaper articles that followed began to appear. See Appendix A (page 100) for this complete document.

D) Councilman Clyde Biglieri

Councilman Biglieri's real estate firm handled the Conforte land transaction and Councilman Biglieri received a large commission from Conforte as a result of the transaction. Thereafter, when he broke the tie vote and cast the decisive vote on the room tax increase, Mr. Biglieri was aware that a substantial portion of the revenue from the tax increase would be used by the Convention Authority to purchase the same land from Conforte and that Conforte was in a position to make major profits from the transaction.

The Grand Jury finds that a conflict of interest existed when Councilman Biglieri voted for the room tax increase. The conflict of interest arose from the Forty Thousand Dollar ($40,000.00) commission that Mr. Biglieri and his associate received from Conforte when Conforte purchased the Capurro property approximately one year earlier.* Also, Councilman Biglieri's action in voting on the room tax increase was obviously inconsistent with his twice earlier voluntary disqualification of himself on the same vote.

* It should be noted that these actions occurred before the criminal conflict of interest law was enacted in the 1975 legislative session and went into effect in July of 1975.

Further considerations relevant to Mr. Biglieri's conflict of interest are that he received a substantial campaign contribution from Joe Conforte, was urged to vote favorably upon the issue by Conforte, and knew he had a chance of receiving extensive Conforte business in connection with the future sale and development of the parcel of land retained by Conforte.

The Grand Jury recommends that public officials assume an affirmative duty to be public watchdogs and alert the public at large when other public officials are involved in unusual transactions. Although he knew of the Drakulich involvement at all times, Councilman Biglieri failed to alert the public to the fact that Drakulich, a State Senator, had received an Eighteen Thousand Dollar ($18,000.00) commission from Joe Conforte when he, Drakulich, had done nothing to earn it.

The newspapers had a field day. They had breaking news, close to home. In the wake of Watergate, they had their own scandal. In a county that didn't allow prostitution, they had possible involvement from Joe Conforte, *the* name in prostitution. They had an elected official they could claim had done something unethical (or at least they thought so) and whose name could easily be connected to Conforte's. The fact that I was never indicted seemed to slip under their radar.

They were on the story. The minute the grand jury report was released, the onslaught of newspaper articles started. The very first article appeared the day after the grand jury report was released and printed the entire 48-page report in the *Nevada State Journal*. The fact that I had not been indicted wasn't brought out in the articles. What *was* brought out was that my name was in the grand jury report.

I found it difficult to lead a normal life. Reporters didn't exactly break down my door or burn up my phone lines – they seemed happy to take the information from any source but me, and there were very few calls from reporters – but the instant and undeserved infamy had an effect. Business dropped precipitously. I found it hard to work. At home I found it hard to relax as I watched the effect the unfolding events and continued articles were having on my wife, Shirley, an effect that wouldn't fully play out until many years later.

Hundreds of articles were published, and overnight my image changed from honorable, hard-working, respected City Councilman to criminal without my ever being indicted. I never have been indicted, and I never hired an attorney for a defense. I didn't need an attorney, and I didn't need to be defended: I didn't do anything wrong. I'd been raised to believe innocence was the only defense needed in America.

I countered in a letter dated March 18, 1976 and asked that the necessary corrections be made to the grand jury report and that the newspapers print retractions and issue a public apology.

In my letter, I brought up the errors in reports of my activities as detailed in the Washoe County Grand Jury Report of March 15, 1976. These errors included:

1. The report stated I received a large commission from Joe Conforte. This is not true. Mr. Conforte never paid Washoe Realty a commission of any sort, whatsoever. The commission, which was paid in full on June 7, 1973, was paid by the sellers.

2. The report stated the commission paid by Conforte later caused a conflict of interest regarding my room tax vote. However, again, Conforte paid no commission. The seller (Capurro) paid the commission, which is the normal procedure in a real estate transaction of this type.

3. The report alleged a conflict of interest existed at the time I voted to approve the room tax increase. I enclosed the opinion from the Nevada Ethics Commission, which clearly stated that I was not in conflict. (AB610, the ethics in government law, had not been enacted at this point, but had it been, I still would not have had a conflict.) My vote came a full 14 months after escrow closed on the property.

4. The report never mentioned that the one-cent room tax increase was instigated by the Chamber of Commerce in its efforts to secure additional revenues for promotional purposes. At the time the room tax increase was proposed by a group from the Chamber of Commerce, several elected public officials and some members of the community had made a survey of a number of convention cities in the West and returned to Reno advocating that the room tax be increased to 6 percent.

In addition to this, the officials of the Chamber of Commerce appeared before the City Council on two occasions in their attempts to get this tax increase approved by the Council. The pursuit of additional revenue was well-publicized by the Reno newspapers.

The letter ended with my reminder that the Fair and Recreation Board changed its priorities to purchase the Conforte land. This was independent action take by that Board, of which I was not a member. I then copied this letter to the Attorney General, *Reno Gazette-Journal*, *Nevada State Journal*, United Press International, KOH Radio, KOLO Radio and the three local television stations.

The letter was never answered. Instead, the contents of my letter made the *Nevada State Journal* March 20, 1976, and simply seemed to spur the media forward.

I would have liked to have laid the matter to rest, but it proved to be impossible. Some 229 articles appeared in local newspapers. Warren Lerude, executive editor of the *Reno Evening Gazette* and *Nevada State Journal*, and Foster Church and Norman Cardoza, both editorial writers for the *Journal* and the *Gazette*, respectively, won a Pulitzer Prize for their editorial writing. Every new article stirred a new spate of print journalism in the matter.

While I wasn't looking to stir things up, I wanted to clear my good name, and I wanted people to listen to me. I'd been falsely accused after going to some length to ensure that everything I did was open and aboveboard. I'd been falsely accused of a conflict of interest after being named in a grand jury report without ever having been indicted. I was smeared.

There was no safe haven. Every part of my life was affected

by the articles and the grand jury report. My business suffered. Eventually Washoe Realty became a one-man show, as business dipped lower and lower. Pulitzer Prize-winning editorials in the newspaper called for me to resign from public office.

My four teenage daughters weren't really affected, according to Carol, my oldest daughter. "He kept it to himself," she says, and while they knew something was going on, they didn't know what, and it wasn't made a part of our household. My wife and I worked hard to keep the scandal out of our girls' lives.

However, that didn't mean my family was safe from everything that was going on. I think it was my wife, Shirley, who was hit the hardest. When accusations and speculation about her husband started and the articles began appearing, Shirley's health began to decline and never recovered from the years of stigma caused by the scandal that never really was.

It's an unlikely story, and it remains unlikely. In 1976, I filed a motion in the Second Judicial District Court, Washoe County, asking that my name be removed from the grand jury report. The court refused. In 1979, I appealed the lower court decision to the Nevada Supreme Court, which handed down a unanimous decision on October 26 ordering that my name be removed from the grand jury report.

**[Pages 37-43] Supreme Court of the State of Nevada – Appeal from Judgment**
In October 1979, the Nevada Supreme Court in a unanimous decision, reversed the decision of the Second Judicial District Court of Nevada, Washoe County, and ordered my name be removed from the grand jury report dated March 15, 1976.

IN THE SUPREME COURT OF THE STATE OF NEVADA

```
CLYDE BIGLIERI,                      )
                                     )
                     Appellant,      )
                                     )
        vs.                          )                    No. 10707
                                     )
WASHOE COUNTY GRAND JURY REPORT      )         FILED
DATED MARCH 15, 1976,                )
                                     )         OCT 25 1979
                     Respondent.)    )
                                     )         CLERK
_____)         By _____ DEPUTY CLERK
```

Appeal from judgment, Second Judicial District Cour
Washoe County; John W. Barrett, Judge.

Reversed and remanded with instructions.

> Steven L. Pevar, American
> Civil Liberties Union,
> Denver, Colorado, and
> Wallace D. Stephens, Reno,
> Nevada,
>              for Appellant.
>
> Calvin R. X. Dunlap, Washoe
> County District Attorney,
> Reno, Nevada,
>              for Respondent.

O P I N I O N

By the Court, MOWBRAY, C.J.:

Clyde Biglieri appeals from the district court's dismissal of his petition to expunge various portions of the Washoe County Grand Jury Report, disseminated on March 15, 1976 Since we agree that those portions of the report were issued in excess of the grand jury's lawful authority under NRS 172.175(3)[1], we reverse.

_____

[1]
   NRS 172.175(3) provides in pertinent part:

   "No report issued pursuant to this section shall single out any person or persons which directly or by innuendo, imputation or otherwise accuses such person or persons of a wrongdoing whi if true would constitute an indictable offense unless the repor is accompanied by a presentment or indictment of such person or persons."

Recently, this Court had occasion to review a simila

petition for expungement brought by Joseph Conforte, one of

the principal targets of the March 15th investigative report.

See In re Washoe County Grand Jury Report, 95 Nev. 121, 590 P.2

622 (1979). At that time, we upheld the constitutionality of

NRS 172.175(2) which empowers the grand jury to investigate and

to report on matters pertaining to the public welfare, morals,

and safety of the community; but we also found that these repor

orial powers are not without limit. Id. at 124, 590 P.2d at

624. For example, a grand jury, when issuing an investigative

report, may not accuse a named individual, either directly or

indirectly, of an indictable offense without returning an indic

ment or presentment. Id. at 125, 590 P.2d at 625; NRS 172.175

In the instant case, appellant concedes that our

opinion in Washoe County effectively disposes of his constituti

attacks on the March 15th report. He insists, however, that

portions of that report, in effect, accuse him of what amounts

criminal activity without giving him the opportunity to respond

to those charges in a judicial forum.[2]  We agree.

Though we have fully detailed the factual background

of the March 15th report in our Washoe County opinion, a brief

summary is in order here.

In July, 1974, the Washoe County Grand Jury commence

an investigation which focused upon a transaction commonly re-

ferred to as the Conforte Land Transaction. The scope of the

---

[2]
Though appellant initially petitioned the district court fo
expungement of the entire grand jury report, he presently seek
expungement only of those portions which single him out
"directly or by innuendo, imputation, or otherwise," of possibl
criminal wrongdoing. We note, in this regard, that appellant
does not have standing to challenge the portions of the report
dealing with other individuals. In re Washoe County Grand Jury
Report, 95 Nev. at 123, 590 P.2d at 624.

-2-

investigation expanded considerably, ultimately involving member
of the Reno and Sparks City Councils, the Washoe County Commissi
and the Washoe Convention Authority. The grand jury publicly
disseminated its report on March 15, 1976.

No presentments or indictments accompanied the report
The grand jury emphasized that "nothing said in this report is
intended to accuse, imply, or create an innuendo that any persor
has committed a criminal offense." Despite this caveat, the
grand jury sharply criticized various named public officials fo1
allegedly breaching their public trust. These named officials,
according to the grand jury, had acted in their official capaci·
ties on matters of public interest without disclosing their con·
flicting personal interests in those matters.

Appellant Biglieri, then a Reno City Councilman, was
one of the officials singled out for criticism in the report.
The grand jury concluded that appellant had performed his official duties with respect to the Conforte Land Transaction and t·
a related city council vote on a proposed room tax increase whi
having a personal stake in the outcome of those matters. The
grand jury based its findings on the following allegations:
appellant's real estate firm had handled the Conforte Land Tran
action and, as a result, appellant had received a large commiss
from Conforte; appellant was aware that a substantial portion o
the revenues raised pursuant to the room tax increase would be
used by the city to purchase a parcel of land from Conforte; ap
pellant knew that Conforte was in a position to reap major prof
from this sale; appellant had received a substantial campaign
contribution from Conforte; appellant was urged by Conforte to
in favor of the proposed room tax increase; appellant had, in 1
cast the tie-breaking vote in favor of the tax increase; and, r
significantly, appellant knew he had a chance of receiving extensive Conforte business in connection with the future sale a1

-3-

development of the parcel of land retained by Conforte. Of cour:
since no indictment was returned, the truth of these allegations
cannot be ascertained.

The question of the validity of these portions of the
March 15th report, unaccompanied by indictment or presentment, i:
now before this Court.

The reportorial function of the grand jury, serving t
enlighten the community on matters of public importance, occupie
an important position in our democratic form of government. We
must be on our guard, however, to distinguish between the grand
jury's power to report upon public affairs and its power to accu
of public offenses. In re Ormsby Grand Jury, 74 Nev. 80, 322 P.
1099 (1958). When singling out an individual through accusation
of possible criminal conduct, the grand jury acts as an inquisit
in its inquisitorial role, the grand jury must either indict or
silent. Id.; NRS 172.175(3). The principle behind this limitat
is quite simply that:

> [A] man should not be made subject to quasi
> official accusation of misconduct which he
> cannot answer in an authoritative forum;
> that in making such accusation the grand
> jury is exceeding its reportorial function
> and is proceeding to impose the punishment
> of reprimand . . . .

In re Ormsby Grand Jury, 74 Nev. at 83, 322 P.2d at 1100; see a]
Nevada State Judiciary Comm., 1973 Legislative Session, Minutes
376 (April 5, 1973) (commenting on the underlying intent of NRS
172.175(3)). In other words, it is one thing for the grand jur;
to find that official acts or practices, although not expressly
forbidden by law, are opposed to the public trust and should be
exposed to public scrutiny; it is quite another thing, however,
for the grand jury "to adjudge such conduct to be morally wrong
or to be misconduct which is censurable or actionable." In re
Ormsby Grand Jury, 74 Nev. at 85-86, 322 P.2d at 1102.

-4-

The dividing line between proper public criticism and unlawful accusations of possible criminal conduct is often difficult to discern, but it is one which must be drawn. The learned district judge below, relying heavily on the fact that Nevada's criminal conflict of interest laws did not take effect until after the dissemination of the grand jury's report and on grand jury's expressed opinion that "[n]othing said in this report is intended to accuse, imply, or create an innuendo that any person has committed a criminal offense," concluded that the report did not accuse appellant of any indictable offenses. We cannot agree. While NRS 245.075, the criminal conflict of inter statute, did not take effect until 1977, we note that NRS 197.110(2), enacted in 1911, makes it a gross misdemeanor for a public officer to "[b]e beneficially interested, directly or indirectly, in any contract, sale, lease or purchase which may b made by, through or under supervision of such officer, in whole or in part . . . ." We find that the grand jury's account of appellant's conduct with respect to the Conforte Land Transactio and the subsequent city council vote on the proposed room tax increase falls squarely within the purview of this statute.

The grand jury, in effect, has accused appellant of official misconduct. If the grand jury had "probable cause" to believe the truth of its allegations relating to appellant's con duct, then the only course consistent with its duty was to retur a presentment or indictment, thereby allowing appellant his day in court to test the truth or falsity of these charges. NRS 172.155(1). If, on the other hand, the grand jury was not satis fied with the accuracy of its information concerning appellant's conduct, then it could report only in general terms on matters pertaining to the public welfare. See NRS 172.175(2) and (3). What the grand jury was not free to do was to suggest that appel lant was guilty of misconduct and then avoid the consequences of its findings by refusing to indict.

-5-

39

Moreover, this Court is not bound by the grand jury own assertion that nothing in its report was intended to accus appellant of criminal activity. If the grand jury could deter mine, free from judicial review, the legal effect of its repor in such a fashion, it would have unlimited opportunity to incl allegations of indictable offenses in violation of NRS 172.175 while, at the same time, immunizing its report from attack by bald statement that those accusations did not amount to wrongd See generally In re Washoe County Grand Jury Report, supra. W decline to grant the grand jury such unfettered power: the gr. jury may not transform its inquiry, in which only the most min safeguards are accorded the subjects of its investigations, se NRS 172.145, into a secret trial culminating in the published condemnation of an individual.

For the above reasons, we reverse the judgment of tl district court and remand the cause with directions to deny respondent's motion for summary judgment and to enter partial summary judgment for appellant, expunging P.26, L.7, through P. L.16, inclusive, from the March 15, 1976 report of the Washoe County Grand Jury.

_____, C.
Mowbray

We concur:

_____, J.
Thompson

_____, J.
Gunderson

_____, J.
Manoukian

BATJER, J. concurring:

The majority opinion sets forth the accusations and allegations against Biglieri contained in the grand jury report. Not one of these allegations could be legitimately used to support an indictment or information for violation of NRS 197.110(2), applying Nevada's probable cause standard. <u>See</u> e.g. Franklin v. State, 89 Nev. 382, 513 P.2d 1252 (1973); State v. von Brincken, 86 Nev. 769, 476 P.2d 733 (1970).

I reluctantly must agree with the majority, however, that there could be an innuendo or imputation of such a violatio Since it appears to be the intent of the Nevada Legislature to render the grand jury impotent in its reporting function, I have no alternative but to concur in the result reached by the majority and conclude that NRS 172.175(3) mandates reversal in this case.

_____, J.
Batjer

The Nevada Supreme Court couldn't order that my life be set right, however.  My reputation was taking a beating, and in 1975 when I ran for re-election to the City Council, one local paper would not endorse me despite the fact that my opponent was in jail and despite my proven track record: I'd spent hundreds of hours working to get the first animal control shelter built in Washoe County, had established what today is Reno's RTC RIDE city bus line, and had worked to get the Reno-Tahoe International Airport on solid ground – after years of operating in the red, the airport was now making money.

I was re-elected in 1975, but by 1979 there was simply too much in print for me to fight against. The newspaper articles were perfect fodder for my opponents, and in 1979 I lost the election, despite my good works.

After the grand jury report, 229 articles appeared in local newspapers about the "scandal."  After the Nevada Supreme Court ordered my name expunged from the grand jury report, clearing me of even a hint of wrongdoing, a total of two articles were printed on the subject.

My problems stemmed largely from the negative press I'd received, including editorial articles (that led to the awarding of a Pulitzer Prize). Some of these articles were written after the *Journal* and *Gazette* had information in their possession that I had done nothing wrong and that the information written about me wasn't true.

The newspapers refused to print a retraction, so I contacted the National News Council and asked them to look into the matter.  The organization had been specifically formed to hear complaints from the public against the media, but after many letters and phone calls, the Council declined to assist me and, not long after (1983), the organization folded.  At the same time, I contacted Columbia Journalism School, the authority for Pulitzer Prizes, talking to two successive directors, but was told Columbia wouldn't hear the complaint because National News Council was already hearing it.

**[Pages 46-47] Columbia Letters**
The correspondence with Columbia University has spanned decades. But the following two letters sum up the argument quite well. I repeatedly appealed to the Pulitzer board's sense of fairness. The board continued to refuse to investigate, though, as seen in the April 12 letter from Sig Gissler, the veracity of my claims was not called into doubt or even cited as a reason for inaction. The board simply did not seem to consider the issue of whether or not the Pulitzer had been awarded for shoddy (or even malicious) reporting worth its time.

COLUMBIA UNIVERSITY IN THE CITY OF NEW YORK

April 12, 2006

# The Pulitzer Prizes
OFFICE OF THE ADMINISTRATOR

Mr. Clyde E. Biglieri
PO Box 911
Reno, NV 89504-0911

Dear Mr. Biglieri:

Your letter to President Lee Bollinger has been referred to this office because the president is only one of 19 members on the Pulitzer Board and has no special authority for handling complaints about past prizes. Indeed, it serves no useful purpose to contact him and, given his heavy duties, you should not expect to hear from him.

That said, I understand your discontent. However, the editorial writing award in question was given 30 years ago and, as my predecessors have told you, this office does not have the time or resources required to investigate your complaint.

All I can suggest is that you contact the current leadership of the newspapers about looking into your longstanding complaint about the editorial and other coverage. Perhaps you can publish a letter to editor stating your side of the matter.

Sincerely,

Sig Gissler
Administrator

April 25, 2006

Columbia University in the City of New York
Office of the President
Lee C. Bollinger
New York City, NY  10027
CERTIFIED MAIL

Dear President Bollinger,

According to Mr. Gissler, you are only one member of the Pulitzer Prize Board, and have no special authority; however, you are also the president of Columbia University. May I suggest that you send the other 18 members of the Pulitzer Board copies of the print materials that I recently sent to you? They could act as a committee as a whole and evaluate my complaint and then you would have a factual consensus of opinion. They will probably suggest what course of action, if any, the board should take. The cost would be minimal and should not take up much of the committee's time. I would be pleased to reimburse Columbia University for copying costs and postage.

Thirty years is a long time for a person to try and clear his name. It is a sad commentary that your predecessor did not properly handle this complaint during his administration. Now it is in your hands, and you can take action or you successor can take care of this matter later on.

As you know, a few years ago Pope John Paul traveled to Israel 60 years after the holocaust and apologized to that nation for the lack of concern by the Vatican for what the Nazis did to the Jews in Europe in the 1930's and 40's. Many times our congress has corrected and apologized for how our leaders treated the Native Americans for hundreds of years. Thousands of times nations, leaders, organizations and individuals have apologized for errors and misspoken words or inappropriate actions. There is nothing wrong in doing what is right.

At the present time I, and several others, are working toward getting a non-fiction book written and published about my life during the past 30 years. If I can accomplish this, I will mail you a copy.

Sincerely,

Clyde E. Biglieri

PO Box 911
Reno, NV  89504-0911
Enc.  Gissler letter 4-12-2006

45

I sought legal means to clear my name. I asked to see the records of my case in early 1979, because the Nevada Real Estate Division had assisted the grand jury in the two-year investigation and because such records should be public record.

It wasn't the first time I'd made the request. In September 1975 I asked Angus McLeod with the Real Estate Division for a copy of the complaint against Washoe Realty. A letter from McLeod in October of that year stated he could find no record of a complaint initiated against Washoe Realty in May 1974. Confused, I wrote back, stating the investigators had referenced Case No. NRED 51074 with the Miranda warning, and also could I see a copy of the letter requesting the Real Estate Division to investigate.

McLeod responded, but the response was negative. My letter had clarified what case I was talking about, but the investigation wasn't closed, and records pertaining to it were not considered open for inspection. I asked to see the name of the person who initiated the action once the investigation closed, but that never happened.

**[Pages 49-51] Letters between Hammond and McLeod**

Letter from James W. Hammond, Jr., executive vice president, Reno Board of REALTORS, Inc., December 10, 1975, requesting clarification from Angus W. McLeod, Real Estate Division, Nevada Department of Commerce, on the new rules regarding how complaints and investigations were handled by the Real Estate Division.
Letter from Hammond to McLeod dated December 19, 1975, asking for clarification of the discretionary power given investigators of the Real Estate Division.
Letter from McLeod to Hammond dated December 23, 1975, stating discretionary powers of investigators of the Nevada Real Estate Division are at the discretion of the investigators, and citing NRS (Nevada Revised Statutes) giving the administrator authority to investigate licensees.

RENO BOARD OF REALTORS, INC.

MEMBER
NATIONAL ASSOCIATION OF REALTORS

*President*
THOMAS M. LEWIS II

*Office*
Lucini & Assoc.
200 E. Liberty
Reno, Nevada 89501
(702) 786-1555

REALTOR

*Executive Vice President*
JAMES W. HAMMOND, JR.

*Board Office:*
400 So. Wells Ave.
Post Office Box 1662
Reno, Nevada 89505
(702) 786-6020

December 10, 1975

Mr. Angus W. McLeod
Real Estate Division
Department of Commerce
State of Nevada
111 W. Telegraph Street
Carson City, Nevada    89701

Dear Mr. McLeod:

Recently we received a copy of the new rules and regulations for Nevada Revised Statute 645 owing to inquiries from our members concerning the scope of investigations in the past, particularly concerning their rights and privileges prior to the filing of a formal complaint, we have a question on procedures.  Specifically, what is the practice past, present, and most importantly, proposed as to informing a potential respondent as to the exact nature of the complaint(s) and the identity of the complainant(s) during the informal phase implied in Section VIII of aforesaid rules and regulations?

We look forward to your reply in order that we may keep our members informed.

Sincerely,

RENO BOARD OF REALTORS, INC.

James W. Hammond, Jr.
Executive Vice President

JWH:ph

*1st Vice President*
J. D. "DICK" LaMAY

*2nd Vice President*
JERALD L. FRANDSEN

*Treasurer*
WILLIAM G. KIMMEL

*Immediate Past President*
WILLIAM H. MYERS, JR.

*CID Chairman*
DAVID A. READ

*Director*
GENE H. BROWN

*Director*
M. W. "BILL" FLEMER

*Director*
GEORGE DOERING

# RENO BOARD OF REALTORS, INC.

**MEMBER**
**NATIONAL ASSOCIATION OF REALTORS**

*President*
THOMAS M. LEWIS II

*Office*
Lucini & Assoc.
230 E. Liberty
Reno, Nevada 89501
(702) 786-1555

REALTOR

*Executive Vice President*
JAMES W. HAMMOND, JR.

*Board Office:*
400 So. Wells Ave.
Post Office Box 1668
Reno, Nevada 89505
(702) 786-6020

December 19, 1975

Mr. Angus W. McLeod
Administrator - Real Estate Division
Department of Commerce, State of Nevada
Administrative Office
Carson City, Nevada 89701

Dear Mr. McLeod:

Thank you for your letter of 17 December 1975 which was generated by my inquiry of 10 December 1975. Although your letter states that procedures are at the discretion of the investigator and by implication, therefore, at the discretion of the Real Estate Division, it does not state whence this discretionary power is derived. I am unable to find a document which I may cite for our members. I would appreciate your assistance on this.

Please forgive me for seeming to belabor a point but my almost twenty-nine years of command and staff experience at all levels in the United States Marine Corps inculcated me with the principle of completed staff work. Hence, I hesitate to go back to the members with only half an answer, especially by virtue of my being new to the position.

Sincerely,

RENO BOARD OF REALTORS, INC.

James W. Hammond, Jr.
Executive Vice President

jwh

**DEPARMENT OF COMMERCE**
**REAL ESTATE DIVISION**
ADMINISTRATIVE OFFICE
CARSON CITY, NEVADA 89701
(702) 885-4280

MIKE O'CALLAGHAN
Governor
MICHAEL L. MELNER
Director
Department of Commerce

ANGUS W. McLEOD
Administrator
Real Estate Division

December 23, 1975

Mr. James W. Hammond, Jr.
Executive Vice President
Reno Board of REALTORS, Inc.
400 South Wells Avenue
Post Office Box 1668
Reno, Nevada   89505

Dear Mr. Hammond:

I have stated in my letter dated, December 17, 1975, that
the procedures used by our Investigators in revealing the
nature and source of the complaint are <u>at the discretion</u>
<u>of the Investigator</u>.  This is not to imply that all inves-
tigative procedures are determined by him.

Each Investigator is familiar with our handbook "The Investigator in Action".  This manual outlines the various tech-
niques which may be employed by the Investigator when investigating a case.

N.R.S. 645.190 gives the Real Estate Division the authority
to do all things necessary for carrying into effect the
provisions of N.R.S. 645.

N.R.S. 645.610 gives the Administrator the authority to
investigate any complaint which involves a licensee.  Therefore, the Administrator is responsible for providing the
guidelines under which our investigations are conducted.

Sincerely,

Jeanne Hannafin
Deputy Administrator

JH:kn

cc:  Angus McLeod

MEMBER: NATIONAL ASSOCIATION OF REAL ESTATE LICENSE LAW OFFICIALS

49

When I asked to see the file against me again in 1979, my request was refused. I was told that if I wanted to see the file, I would have to initiate a court action. So I did. Then a few days before the trial date, the division destroyed the file. So there was no trial.

**[Below] Letter from me to Angus McLeod, Real Estate administrator, State of Nevada]**
Letter to Angus McLeod, real estate administrator, State of Nevada regarding the May 15, 1974, visit to Washoe
Realty by Real Estate Division investigators Laqua and Baumann, requesting the chance to see a copy of the
complaint. There was never any answer to this letter.

Reno, Nevada
September 19, 1975

Mr. Angus McCleod
Real Estate Administrator
State of Nevada
111 West Telegraph
Carson City, Nevada

Dear Mr. McCleod:

On May 15, 1974, Real Estate Division Investigators
Laqua and Rovetti appeared in my office and asked to see
my files and also to discuss the Capurro-Conforte land
sale in Washoe County, Nevada.

This investigation came as a complete surprise as no one
from the Real Estate Division had made a prior call or
written to request time for a interview. I asked these
state officials who had filed a complaint; the sellers,
Capurro or the buyer Conforte? Neither of them would
answer this question but assured me that there was a
complaint on file with Mr. Skip Hansen, the then
Commissioner in Carson City, Nevada. They did not have a
copy in their possession when I asked to see the complaint.
I immediately tried to contact Mr. Hansen in Carson City
but his secretary told me Mr. Hansen was in Las Vegas
and could not be reached. His secretary, upon questioning,
said that she had seen the complaint and Mr. Hansen
had it with him. She also said she could not remember
the name of the person filing the complaint.

I realize it is a little late to ask for this information .
but my curiosity has gotten the best of me. Would you
please honor my request and furnish me a copy of the
complaint filed against Washoe Realty during the month of
May, 1974.

Sincerely yours,

Clyde E. Bigleri
Washoe Realty

The files were destroyed, officials in the Real Estate Division told me, because the division was making room in its warehouse. But curiously, only a few files were destroyed, one of which happened to contain the information pertaining to my case.

**[Pages 54-55]** *Nevada Appeal* **article dated February 1979 regarding destruction of Nevada Real Estate Division Biglieri files.**
On February 14 and 15, 1979, the *Nevada Appeal* and *Reno Gazette-Journal* printed articles regarding the Nevada Real Estate Division destroying the files in my case. According to Jeanne Hannafin, division deputy administrator, the files were destroyed four days after she notified my attorney that I would not be allowed to examine the files without a court order. (I hired the attorney to try to get my file; I never hired anyone to prove my innocence. I didn't feel I had to.) She claimed the timing was a simple coincidence, the destruction being a part of a routine procedure for getting rid of outdated materials.

# Real estate investiga

## Reno councilman sought information

By SUSAN MANUEL
Appeal Staff Writer

The day before Reno Councilman Clyde Biglieri was to go to court to force the Nevada Real Estate Division to show him material gathered on him during an investigation, he found the division's investigative file on him had been destroyed.

At the hearing Wednesday the state was to produce the file under a writ of mandamus filed by Biglieri's attorney Bob Grayson.

But Robert Herman, attorney for the Real Estate Division, said the proceedings were moot, because the file no longer existed.

Biglieri wanted to know what the state gathered on him

during a 1973-74 investigation of a land sale involving his real estate firm, brothel owner Joe Conforte and the Reno-Sparks Convention Authority.

Biglieri filed suit because he said he was never informed of charges against him and he was refused copies of complaints against him, as well as other relevant documents.

Wednesday, under questioning by Grayson, Jean Hanifin, former deputy administrator of the Real Estate Division, said she ordered the file destroyed, along with several others.

Whether by coincidence or not, her orders came four days after she wrote Biglieri's attorney, Denis Fealy, that he could see the file only with a court order.

Hanifin's testimony was significant in Grayson's attempt to

Handwritten notes in margin: from Carson City Library / Feb 15 79 / New Appeal

**NEVADA APPEAL** — Carson

# ...tion files destroyed

## ...gathered during probe into land deal

...show the files were "improperly destroyed."

Hanifin said that last summer her department decided to destroy all investigative files dated prior to July 1974. Files not destroyed were those with some action taken on the investigations; those which contained matters pending in court; and those with investigations of land sale companies continuing because of ongoing complaints.

As far as she knew, Hanifin said, the investigation of the Biglieri "incident" was completed before she was employed by the department.

There were no "formal complaints" made against Biglieri, she said, and no actions taken.

Hanifin said many files were destroyed, but that she didn't know whether Biglieri's was among them.

However, investigator Marvin Laqua, who kept the Biglieri file from 1974 until he shredded it by hand in August 1978, said Hanifin specifically told him to destroy the Biglieri file.

Attorney Grayson made a motion to amend his writ of mandamus so that he could interview in camera witnesses who would know what the destroyed file might have contained. His original writ had been to examine the file.

Judge Michael Griffin said that under the law people could not be compelled to testify with the present writ. The judge denied the motion "without prejudice," and suggested Grayson seek another route.

Grayson said after the hearing he would examine the alternatives, but didn't know what he and Biglieri do next.

# marksmen suggest way

53

At the moment the investigators, Laqua and Baumann, walked into Washoe Realty and asked to see the file on the Capurro-Conforte transaction, my life began to change. It's never been the same. Over the years I lost my good name, my business, my seat on the City Council, and eventually, I lost the woman I'd been married to for 51 years. Shirley's health continued to fail over the years, and doctors stated they believed the strain of the never-ending situation, the negative publicity and the false accusations leveled against her husband, finally took their toll.

I have spent a good deal of time thinking about this mess that took up so much time and caused so much pain in my life. I have tried to see it from all angles. Sure, maybe it was all an innocent mistake. Maybe I *was* falsely accused and no one was able to help me clear my name because every step had really been taken in good faith, and the train *still* went off the tracks. It could happen, I guess. Everyone with the power to make decisions *could've* suddenly lost the power to help. Everyone who was supposed to be checking the facts *could* have fallen asleep at the wheel. It *could* all be a big misunderstanding. But it's not likely.

Of course, the Conforte "connection" needs to be considered. I have talked to Conforte less than half a dozen times in my life. During my first run for City Council in 1971, I was introduced to Joe Conforte by mutual friends and received an unsolicited $500 campaign contribution, which differentiates me not at all from most politicians at the time: Conforte was a businessman in Nevada with an interest in local politics. I didn't report the contribution because I didn't have to – the campaign contributions law didn't go into effect in Nevada until 1975. When I stated in the grand jury hearing that I'd received a campaign contribution from Conforte, it was hardly a smoking gun.

However, it was as close to malfeasance as the grand jury could get. The sale of the land from Capurro to Conforte, which was, in itself, a legitimate transaction, was performed by Jimmy Smith through Washoe Realty because Smith had sold property to Conforte when he had worked for another real estate agency – Smith and Conforte knew each other; that was it. One professional simply turned to another whose expertise he trusted.

While there is evidence that there was political corruption among Conforte and a few select elected officials, that did not mean everyone who ever did business with Conforte should be painted with the same brush. For good or ill, Conforte was a legitimate businessman, and many of his business dealings were simply part of doing legal business. He purchased business supplies, he hired repairmen and accountants, he made charitable donations, and, yes, he bought and sold land. Not everyone Conforte did business with was corrupt. The grand jury had been part of a fishing expedition that was honestly meant to clean up the town. But the net was cast too wide, and I, for one, got wrongly caught in it.

However, the name Conforte is redolent of prostitution and politics, and in 1974 the Washoe County District Attorney's Office, the *Nevada State Journal* and the *Reno Evening Gazette,* and the Organized Crime Unit, a federally-funded, county-wide law enforcement agency, were working together, trying to bring Conforte down. They'd been looking for a long time, pushing different ways to get at Conforte, and if I got caught in the crossfire, that was just too bad.

# BEHIND THE SCENES

On March 16, 1976, the Nevada Real Estate Advisory Commission convened a hearing in Nevada's state capital, Carson City, with James W. Hammond, Jr., personally appearing. The hearing was to discuss investigative procedures used by the Real Estate Division during the informal portion of an investigation or, in other words, how the investigators should have acted when they visited Washoe Realty in 1974.

In addition to Hammond, who was the executive vice president of the Reno Board of REALTORS, Inc., four members of the commission were present, along with the counsel for the commission, Bob Edmondson. Jeanne Hannafin for the Division, was present, along with the counsel for the Division; Angus McLeod was also at the meeting with Investigators Laqua and Baumann and other individuals.

**[Pages 58-94] Minutes from the Nevada Real Estate Advisory Commission**
Minutes from the Nevada Real Estate Advisory Commission regarding investigative procedures, March 16, 1976. Individuals involved in the investigation by Nevada Real Estate Division Investigators Laqua and Baumann met to discuss how complaints against individual REALTORS and brokers were handled and where the discretionary authority of the division and its investigators came from.

Many details came to light in this hearing, including the fact that while I was never allowed to see the complaint against Washoe Realty or the letter directing the investigators to investigate, there was a case number assigned. Also that I had never been allowed to examine the file, which Nevada Real Estate Division personnel stated was because the case was still open and being investigated at the time of my request.

Also discussed was the appearance of a connection between the investigating body and the Washoe County Sheriff's Office Organized Crime Unit.

1                NEVADA REAL ESTATE ADVISORY COMMISSION

2  SUBJECT:   Investigative Procedures Used By the Real Estate

3              Division During the Informal Portion of An Investigation

4  THOSE       Bob Hass           John Gibbons
   PRESENT:   Betty Krolak       Marion Rovetti

5              Fred Schultz       Buck Baumann
               Olivia Silvagni    Jim Barnes

6              Bob Edmondson    Clyde Biglieri
               Angus McLeod     James W. Hammond, Jr.

7              Jeanne Hannafin   Jackie Butler
               Norma Woolverton  Shirley Miller

8              Kathy Noland     Tom Lewis
               Marv Laqua       Bill Myers

9

10  HASS:     This is the time and place set for a personal appearance

11          by James W. Hammond, Jr., Executive Vice President, Reno

12          Board of REALTORS, Inc. Those in attendance on the

13          Commission are: Fred Schultz, Betty Krolak, Olivia

14          Silvagni and myself, Bob Hass. The counsel to the

15          Commission, Bob Edmondson, is here. For the Division:

16          Jeanne Hannafin; counsel to the Division, Jim Barnes;

17          Angus McLeod; Mr. Gibbons and Marv Laqua; Buck Baumann;

18          Norma Woolverton. Does that cover everybody? So, Mr.

19          Hammond, would you care to take the floor. If you want

20          to, you can sit down.

21  HAMMOND:  Well, I think I talk better on my feet, thank you.

22  HASS:     Go right ahead.

23  HAMMOND:  I'm both a stand up talker and a stand up drinker. It

24          makes it go down easier. I'm Wes Hammond, I'm the

25          Executive Vice President, of the Reno Board of REALTORS

26          and have been since 8, September, 1975. I think I

27          should preface my remarks by saying I am not a licensed

28          real estate salesman or broker as a matter of fact, my

29          only experience in the real estate field is when I

30          bought my first house last August. Which was a delight-

31          ful experience by the way. Nor am I an attorney, but

32          I'm here to seek some answers that I have not been able

HAMMOND:   to get by correspondence in a dialogue and I don't fully
expect to get a definitive answer here today, but I
certainly would like to continue the dialogue and show
exactly what the questions are that have been addressed
to me by our members. As you know, we have well over
500 members of our Board in Reno.   538 as of the last
count.   At the direction, after several inquiries, at
the direction of our board of directors on 10 December,
I addressed a letter to the Real Estate Division which
if I may read:   "Recently we received a copy of the new
rules and regulations for the Nevada Revised Statute 645.
Owing to inquiries from our members concerning the scope
of investigations in the past, particularly concerning
their rights and privileges prior to the filing of a
formal complaint, we have a question on procedures.
Specifically, what is the practice past, present, and
most importantly, proposed as to informing a potential
respondent as to the exact nature of the complaint,
complaints, and the identity of the complaint, complainants during the informal phase implied in Section VIII
of aforesaid rules and regulations?   We look forward to
your reply in order that we may keep our members informed."   Signed by me.   17 December, letter from the Real
Estate Division:   "Dear Mr. Hammond, In answer to your
letter December 10, 1975, inquiring as to our procedures
in revealing the nature of the complaint or the identity
of the complainant, it would be fair to say that the
practice varies depending on the case.   For the most
part, it is at the discretion of the investigator who
is assigned to the case.   There are instances in which
the consumer has requested that his identity not be revealed.   We try to conduct our investigation in such a

-2-

1  HAMMOND:    manner as to gather factual information regarding the

2                   transaction, and if in the opinion of the Division,

3                   there is insufficient evidence to warrant a formal com-

4                   plaint, the case is closed. All cases are confidential,

5                   and not public information." I'd like to come back to

6                   that in a second. "They can be obtained by securing a

7                   court subpoena. In the event that a formal complaint is

8                   filed with the Advisory Commission, the case goes to a

9                   public hearing, a transcript is obtained, and that be-

10                 comes public record along with the Finding of Fact. In

11                 most instances there is a consumer complaint, the inves-

12                 tigator does reveal the identity of the complainant, and

13                 the nature of the complaint as it frequently helps him

14                 to expedite the investigation. There are times when it

15                 would be in the best interest of all parties concerned

16                 not to reveal this information, and the investigator is

17                 permitted to proceed in whatever manner he prefers. Hope

18                 this answers your questions, and if I can be of any fur-

19                 ther assistance, please do not hesitate to call me.

20                 Sincerely, Jeanne Hannafin, Deputy Administrator for

21                 Angus McLeod, Administrator." Whereupon I replied on

22                 the 19th of December. "Dear Mr. McLeod: Thank you for

23                 your letter of 17 December which was generated by my

24                 inquiry of 10 December, 1975. Although your letter

25                 states the procedures are at the discretion of the inves-

26                 tigator and by implication, therefore, at the discretion

27                 of the Real Estate Division, it does not state whence

28                 this discretionary power is derived. I am unable to find

29                 a document which I may cite for our members. I would

30                 appreciate your assistance on this. Please forgive me

31                 for seeming to belabor a point but my almost twenty-nine

32                 years command of staff experience at all levels in the

-3-

| | |
|---|---|
| 1 | HAMMOND: United States Marine Corps inculcated me with the |
| 2 | principle of completed staff work. Hence, I hesitate to |
| 3 | go back to the members with only half an answer, espe- |
| 4 | cially by my virtue of being new to the position." 23rd |
| 5 | December, "Dear Mr. Hammond: As I, I stated in my letter |
| 6 | December 17th, 1975, the procedures used by our investi- |
| 7 | gators in revealing the nature and source of the com- |
| 8 | plaint are at the discretion of the investigator. This |
| 9 | is not to imply that all investigative procedures are |
| 10 | determined by him. Each investigator is familiar with |
| 11 | our handbook, the title of which is The Investigator In |
| 12 | Action. This manual outlines the various techniques |
| 13 | which may be employed by the investigator when investi- |
| 14 | gating a case. N.R.S. 645.190 gives the Real Estate |
| 15 | Division the authority to do all things necessary for |
| 16 | carrying into effect the provisions of N.R.S. 645. |
| 17 | N.R.S. 645.610 gives the Administrator the authority to |
| 18 | investigate any complaint which involves a licensee. |
| 19 | Therefore, the Administrator is responsible for provid- |
| 20 | ing the guidelines under which our investigations are |
| 21 | conducted. Sincerely." Well, I cited those, I checked |
| 22 | those two citations and 6190 says the Real Estate Divi- |
| 23 | sion may do all things necessary and proper for carrying |
| 24 | into effect the provisions of this chapter. The Commis- |
| 25 | sion or the Administrator, with the approval of the Com- |
| 26 | mission, may from time to time adopt reasonable regula- |
| 27 | tions for the administration of this chapter in compli- |
| 28 | ance with the Nevada Administrative Procedure Act which |
| 29 | regulations are proposed by the Administrator in addi- |
| 30 | tion to other notices required by law. He shall provide |
| 31 | copies of the proposed regulation to the Commission no |
| 32 | less than thirty days prior to the next Commission |

-4-

60

| | |
|---|---|
| 1 | HAMMOND: |

HAMMOND: meeting. The Commission shall approve, amend or dis-
approve any proposed regulations at such meeting. All
regulations adopted by the Commission or whether adopted
by the Administrator with the approval of the Commission
shall be published by the Division and offered for sale
at a reasonable fee. The Real Estate Division may
publish a reference manual, a study manual for licensees,
applicants for license and may offer for sale at a reasonable fee. I have a question then on the, my inquiry
where it stopped by a reference to the NRS thing did not
offer the details of what this published regulation by
the Division is and for sale at a reasonable fee. I do
not have a copy of that. There is one other thing that
applies as I said I'd go back. All cases are confidential and are not public information. 645.620, Real
Estate Division to maintain record of complaints, investigations etc. The Real Estate Division shall maintain
in its main office a public docket or other record in
which it shall record from time to time, as made, the
rulings of decisions upon all complaints filed with it.
All investigations instituted by it in the first instance or upon, upon or in connection with which any
hearing shall have been heard or the licensee charged
shall have made no defense.

My basic question is, getting back to my initial letter
of the 10th of December. What are the rights of a
particular licensee as to, as we all know in criminal
cases, and I'm certainly not talking about criminal
cases, but I think that the celebrated Miranda-type
decision which everything flowed requires that anybody
who is a suspect or accused has a right to know who is

| | | |
|--|--|--|
| 1 | HAMMOND: | making the complaint, the nature of the complaint and |
| 2 | | his questioner. My basic question then, rephrasing it, |
| 3 | | is do these same things obtain when applied to a licensee |
| 4 | | particularly to our members because that's the ones that |
| 5 | | I have an answer to. Thats all. |
| 6 | HASS: | Is that is, Mr. Hammond? |
| 7 | HAMMOND: | Thank you. |
| 8 | HASS: | Anyone wish to, from the Division wish to respond or is |
| 9 | | there someone else wish to amplify on Mr. Hammond's |
| 10 | | statements. |
| 11 | LEWIS: | My name is Tom Lewis, I'm President of the Reno |
| 12 | HASS: | Excuse me Mr. Lewis, I'd like the record to show that |
| 13 | | Marion Rovetti has entered the room from the Division. |
| 14 | LEWIS: | Tom Lewis. I'm here as President of the Reno Board of |
| 15 | | REALTORS. This subject matter came to us from an inquiry |
| 16 | | from one of our members, Clyde Biglieri who had been |
| 17 | | approached by some investigators from the Real Estate |
| 18 | | Division. He wasn't satisfied with the, his contact |
| 19 | | with the investigators and the manner in which they |
| 20 | | approached his office and tried to get some answers and |
| 21 | | couldn't seem to, and he asked our board to look into |
| 22 | | what as Mr. Hammond has explained, and I have a further |
| 23 | | question beyond Mr. Hammond or a suggestion beyond Mr. |
| 24 | | Hammond that there seems to be a lack here of communica- |
| 25 | | tion or understanding between the Administrator's office |
| 26 | | and what NRS 645.190 and 610 indicate how the operation |
| 27 | | of these investigations go. The NRS's seem to clearly |
| 28 | | indicate that the procedures are set for by, or at least |
| 29 | | with the approval of, the Advisory Commission. Whereas, |
| 30 | | the letters to our board in response to Mr. Hammond's |
| 31 | | correspondence indicated that they are at the discretion |
| 32 | | of the Administrator's office and this seems to be the |

-6-

LEWIS:   area that we are concerned with is because of the manner
which the investigators approached one of our member,
and we could not seem to find any documentation that,
and still can't, that they were able to approach him in
the manner in which they did.  Because everything leads
back to the fact that rules and regulations are subject
to final judgment on them by this Commission.  It also
states as Mr. Hammond said that these rules and regulations once they are established outside of NRS's will be
published and will be available for sale so that people
will know what the rules of the ballgame are if they get
involved.  Again we don't have any knowledge at least in
our board of this publication that was referred to in one
of the correspondence nor was it suggested that we could
get one or that there was one for sale which indicated the
methods of operation by the investigators.  Once this
one question came up several other board members had the
same, have had the same problem in the past and brought
it to our attention so we felt as a board, and as Mr.
Hammond indicated authorized by our directors, would come
to get a clarification as to in actual practice and in
relation to NRS's where does the authorization for the
methods and the procedures in regulations of the investigators stem from and how is it being practiced and if
there is an ambiguity in this area then we would request
that the Commission assert its prerogatives and its
position under the NRS's to stipulate what these rules
and regulations should be and make them available so that
all licensees will know what they are and know what their
rights are and how they should react and proceed when
investigators come into their office.  Clyde is also
here to give some specifics on his particular case to

-7-

| | | |
|---|---|---|
| 1 | LEWIS: | give you a better idea of exactly what we are talking |
| 2 | | about in specifics. |
| 3 | HASS: | Thank you, Mr. Lewis.  Clyde. |
| 4 | BIGLIERI: | Mr. Chairman also members of the Commission my name is |
| 5 | | Clyde Biglieri.  I own the Washoe Realty Company in Reno, |
| 6 | | Nevada, located at 1100 Kietzke Lane and with your per- |
| 7 | | mission, I would rather sit than stand because I'm going |
| 8 | | to refer to some information that I have in a file.  To |
| 9 | | get into the meat of the subject that Mr. Hammond and |
| 10 | | Mr. Lewis brought up, I would like to read from notes |
| 11 | | that I made during the middle of the year 1974 and they |
| 12 | | are just rough notes and I'll refer to them and talk |
| 13 | | along as I go along so that I can give you an outline of |
| 14 | | the case that I am specifically interested in for my own |
| 15 | | personal benefit. |
| 16 | | |
| 17 | | On Wednesday, May 15th, 1974 at 10:30 a.m. Marvin Laqua |
| 18 | | and Ms. Rovetti both investigators for the Department |
| 19 | | of Commerce, Real Estate Division called at Washoe Realty |
| 20 | | and asked to see me.  I showed them into my office and |
| 21 | | asked what I could do for them.  They said that they |
| 22 | | wanted to discuss the Capurro-Conforte transaction.  They |
| 23 | | asked to see the file and I gave it to them.  Then they |
| 24 | | asked for me to give them the story about the sale.  I |
| 25 | | said that I would do this and then called in Mr. Smith |
| 26 | | into my office and introduced the parties.  I explained |
| 27 | | to Smith what the investigators wanted and he also agreed |
| 28 | | to tell them his version of the sale.  Mr. Laqua said |
| 29 | | that he wanted to hear my version of the transaction |
| 30 | | first and Smith's later.  I requested that we do this at |
| 31 | | a later time as I had to attend a meeting with the com- |
| 32 | | mittee which I chair and was handling the negotiations |

-8-

1 BIGLIERI: with the airlines for landing fees at the Reno Inter-
2 national Airport. The investigators asked Smith to give
3 his story and he said he would rather wait till I gave
4 mine first as I was the broker. We agreed that we would
5 reserve Friday morning for them May the 17th, 1974 and
6 give the investigators all the time that they wanted to
7 hear our story at that time.

9 Friday, May the 17th, 1974 9:00 a.m. I walk into my
10 office and Mr. Laqua was waiting along with Mr. Baumann
11 who is also an investigator for the Real Estate Division.
12 I asked Mr. Baumann if I could see a copy of the com-
13 plaint, because in the past whenever an investigator
14 showed up at our office they always had a complaint with
15 them. We were allowed to see it and respond accordingly.
16 He said that he did not have one. I then asked them if
17 this was customary to investigate if neither the buyer
18 or seller had filed a complaint. Mr. Laqua said the
19 Administrator had ordered them to investigate the sale.
20 Skip Hansen was the Administrator at that time. I then
21 asked if I could see his order, they said that they did
22 not have a letter from him but there was a letter on file
23 with another person asking the department to investigate.
24 I asked who the third person was and Laqua said he didn't
25 know. I then picked up the phone and called the Real
26 Estate Division in Carson City and talked with Mr.
27 Hansen's secretary. She said that Mr. Hansen was out of
28 town, and she would look for the letter on file. After
29 a few minutes she told me she couldn't find the letter
30 and referred me to Mr. Bob Edmondson who is with the
31 Attorney General's office and assigned to the Real Estate
32 Division. I called Mr. Edmondson and asked about the

-9-

1 BIGLIERI: letter. He said Hansen had it with him in his pocket. He
2       said that the Administrator has the right to investigate
3       anything he wants to. I agreed and again asked why, and
4       who signed the letter on file. He would not tell me or
5       even let me know what the contents of the letter was. I
6       asked if I sent in twenty-five complaints for them to
7       investigate if they would do it, and he said yes. I said
8       that I thought that would be a waste of the taxpayer's
9       money. I said why are you investigating this matter? He
10      said, Edmondson, haven't you been reading the paper late-
11      ly? This was the time that all this hit the paper about
12      the room tax vote and the sale to Capurro and Conforte.
13 EDMONDSON: Something recent was in there
14 BIGLIERI: I said yes I'd been reading the paper, but what has that
15      got to do with the Commission investigating this sale.
16      He said they can investigate what they wanted. I again
17      agreed but asked to see a letter of authorization from
18      someone to investigate Washoe Realty. The conversation
19      ended shortly after this. Mr. Laqua then said can we
20      proceed with the interview. I said yes. He then pro-
21      duced a waiver for me to sign which this is a copy of
22      here, and you people might have one, is a copy of the
23      Miranda Decision, when you arrest a person you read him
24      their rights, typed over on the State of Nevada station-
25      ery and I could let you look at this if you haven't seen
26      it. Where am I at now? I read it over and said that I
27      would not sign it and asked why the waiver? He said he
28      needed it to proceed. I very strongly protested and said
29      that in the past when the investigators had a complaint
30      filed against my firm I was allowed to see and read the
31      complaint before I answered and then always complied with
32      the investigation one hundred percent. Laqua said, "you,

-10-

1  BIGLIERI: if you won't sign, there is no reason for us to stay."

2  He put away his briefcase and walked to the other end of

3  the building where Mr. Smith's office is located.  And I

4  want to say that we had some pretty sharp words about

5  this time and, that I didn't type up how I told them and

6  what they could do with the Miranda Decision because I

7  wasn't going to sign it under no conditions.  I just

8  couldn't see it.  Anyone could walk in and ask you to

9  sign your rights away with no background, nothing what-

10  soever.  So we had some very harsh words.  So we walked

11  down to the other end of the building where Mr. Smith's

12  has his desk.  I told Mr. Smith what had happened in my

13  office and advised him of my actions, told him to use

14  his own judgment in talking with the investigators.  Mr.

15  Smith asked Laqua four times to see the waiver so he

16  could read it over before he would say if he would sign

17  it or not.  Smith read it over and said he would not sign

18  it.  Laqua said that we had agreed to give them a state-

19  ment.  We said that was true and we would give them all

20  the time they needed, but we were not going to sign the

21  waiver.  Laqua then asked if I would give him a state-

22  ment.  Let him write it down and sign it.  I said I would

23  not.  I said you can write it down and you can sign it,

24  whatever you want, but I'm not going to sign it.  He said

25  "why not?"  I said what if your briefcase is stolen or

26  lose the matter and it ends up in the newspaper.  He was

27  quite indignant and said that I was implying that he

28  would leak the information.  I objected to him inter-

29  pretating my statement.  Mr. Laqua then called Carson

30  City and talked with Mr. Edmondson and told Edmondson

31  that we would not sign the waiver.  Edmondson apparently

32  then told Laqua to listen to our story as we had

-11-

67

1 BIGLIERI: originally agreed to. I then told the investigators if
2 they wanted to call the Sheriff's Department, I would
3 go down there with them and sign a release which would
4 give the investigators permission to read the sworn
5 statement that I had given to the Sheriff's Department.
6 He said no he didn't want to do that. This time I told
7 the investigators that when we gave our sworn statement
8 we were not asked to sign the waiver nor were we asked
9 to sign it. Smith concurred with my statement. He said
10 we would be willing to give a sworn statement to the
11 Real Estate Division, but would not sign a waiver. Laqua
12 then said let us hear your story and I told it to him
13 and Baumann. Smith then met with them individually,
14 privately, and told them his story and they left shortly
15 before lunch.
16
17 Now that happened in May of 74 and I sort of let things
18 happen. I think you might and I'm not tying this state-
19 ment that I'm making here to you this morning, this
20 afternoon, in any way, shape, manner or form to what was
21 appeared in the Nevada State Journal this morning, but
22 might possibly be related to that. How, I have no way
23 of knowing that. So I talked with Skip Hansen and he
24 wrote me a letter with no date on it. So I don't know
25 even know when this happened. But, I asked him one time
26 about the investigation. He wrote this letter back, but
27 then this started up again and (comment while shuffling
28 papers). Well in September about that time Mr. Chairman
29 I initiated the action again to the Division but I want
30 to know who filed that complaint. I think that I am
31 entitled to that, the right under the Constitution of
32 the United State of America and still am getting the

-12-

1  BIGLIERI: shuffle so Okay let me read this. Thank you very much
2            Wes has it in his place. It says "Dear Mr. McLeod:
3            dated September the 19th, 75. On May 15th, 1974, Real
4            Estate Division Investigators Laqua and Rovetti appeared
5            in my office and asked to see my files and also to dis-
6            cuss the Capurro-Conforte land sale in Washoe County,
7            Nevada. This investigation came as a complete surprise
8            as no one from the Real Estate Division had made a prior
9            call or written to request time for an interview. I
10           asked these state officials who filed a complaint, the
11           sellers, Capurro or the buyer Conforte? Neither of them
12           would answer the question but assured me that there was
13           a complaint on file with Mr. Skip Hansen, who was the
14           Commissioner in Carson City, at that time. They did not
15           have a copy in their possession when I asked to see the
16           complaint. I immediately tried to contact Mr. Hansen in
17           Carson City but his secretary told me Mr. Hansen was in
18           Las Vegas and could not be reached. His secretary, upon
19           questioning said that she had seen the complaint and Mr.
20           Hansen had it with him. She also said she could not
21           remember the name of the person filing the complaint. I
22           realize it is a little late to ask for this information
23           but my curiosity has gotten the best of me. Would you
24           please honor my request and furnish me a copy of the
25           complaint filed against Washoe Realty during the month
26           of May, 1974." Now I have a letter back from
27  HAMMOND:  Should be
28  BIGLIERI: Okay, you have a more accurate file than I do. No, you
29            don't have them all.
30  HAMMOND:  No, those are the agenda items for October, I believe.
31  BIGLIERI: Oh, I've got it here. Is that the 24th?
32  HAMMOND:  Yea.

-13-

1 BIGLIERI: I've got that. Complaint filed against Washoe Realty
2 24th of 75. "Dear Mr. Biglieri: Any information per-
3 taining to an investigation that the Real Estate Division
4 would have in its possession prior to filing a complaint
5 with the Advisory Commission would be strictly confiden-
6 tial. However, I can find no record of a complaint being
7 initiated against Washoe Realty in May of 1974. Signed
8 by Angus McLeod." October the first, 1975, from me to
9 McLeod. "Thank you for your immediate response to my
10 letter of September 19, 75 wherein I requested a copy of
11 the complaint filed against Washoe Realty in 1974.
12 According to your letter to me there is not a complaint
13 against Washoe Realty in your files pertaining to the
14 Capurro-Conforte land sale. Now I am really confused.
15 When the Real Estate Division Investigators were in my
16 office in May of 1974, they asked me to sign a waiver,
17 (copy attached) which I refused to do. This waiver is
18 numbered Case No. NRED vs. 51074. Would you please let
19 me know the status of this case. Additionally, if there
20 is a letter requesting the Real Estate Division to inves-
21 tigate the Capurro-Conforte sale, I feel that I am en-
22 titled to have a copy of this letter and am now request-
23 ing same. Thank you for any consideration you give to
24 this request." McLeod to Biglieri, October 7th. "This
25 letter responds to yours of October first. The Division
26 has no complaint against Washoe Realty, but your letter
27 identifying the case number NRED vs. 51074 did help us
28 in identifying the complaint previously referred to.
29 This investigation is not closed and the records per-
30 taining thereto are not open for inspection." Back to
31 McLeod, "According to your letter, October 28th, accord-
32 ing to your letter of October 7th, there is a current

-14-

| | | |
|---|---|---|
| 1 | BIGLIERI: | and open investigation by the Real Estate Division of |
| 2 | | Washoe Realty concerning the Capurro-Conforte land sale. |
| 3 | | As you know, I am quite concerned with this investiga- |
| 4 | | tion. And when the investigation is concluded, I would |
| 5 | | certainly appreciate knowing the name of the person who |
| 6 | | initiated the action. Please keep this request in mind |
| 7 | | and when the case is closed, I will like to be so |
| 8 | | advised." Well six hundred days have lapsed approximate- |
| 9 | | ly, and we still, I can't find out if there is a com- |
| 10 | | plaint or where it come from and I am, went to the Board |
| 11 | | of REALTORS in Reno and told them of my plight and asked |
| 12 | | their help as a member of the board and they discussed |
| 13 | | this at one of their board meetings and agreed to pursue |
| 14 | | this matter further which they have done through the |
| 15 | | correspondence with Mr. Hammond as Hammond has outlined |
| 16 | | to you people. So that's where we're at right now. I |
| 17 | | feel myself that after six hundred days of a case being |
| 18 | | open in the Division and if I'm not mistaken the law says |
| 19 | | that in ninety days or something like that you are either |
| 20 | | suppose to file a charge or dismiss it. Well, we've gone |
| 21 | | over that by five hundred and ten days approximately, and |
| 22 | | still nobody will answer a question. Nobody will tell me |
| 23 | | about the complaint, so I'm just here myself for some |
| 24 | | information gathering and would like you to consider this |
| 25 | | request formal, and my appearance here is, I be allowed |
| 26 | | to see that file. |
| 27 | HASS: | Well, we've heard the name of Mr. McLeod and maybe Mr. |
| 28 | | Edmondson mentioned here. Somebody |
| 29 | McLEOD: | I'll say, I'll start off by saying that perhaps Jeanne |
| 30 | | would want to talk more about whats in our letters. I |
| 31 | | think that our letters are pretty self-explanatory. |
| 32 | | That's our position. As a sideline, I did discuss this |

-15-

| | |
|---|---|
| 1 | McLEOD: |
| 2 | |
| 3 | |
| 4 | |
| 5 | |
| 6 | HASS: |
| 7 | EDMONDSON: |

1  McLEOD:    whole situation with Paul Argeres and Bill Cozart a

2                couple of weeks ago and they are entirely in support of

3                our procedures in the investigation.  They want to make

4                it very clear that this effort here is not supported by

5                the State Association.

6  HASS:        Well, was there ever a complaint?

7  EDMONDSON:  Can I, perhaps I can set the stage here.  Some of the

8                citations read to you, maybe the force and effect of the

9                language escaped you, but I'm going to read it again.

10              One of the provisions, 645.610 the Administrator may upon

11              his own motion and shall upon the complaint in writing

12              of any person investigate the actions of any real estate

13              broker, real estate salesman.  If I recall right, I read

14              you that section when you talked to me on the phone.

15              What that means is that the Administrator has full

16              authority to investigate on his own with or without any

17              piece of paper to start with.  I mean that's clear.  As

18              you are well aware at that time the Sheriff's office was

19              investigating the transaction as we've recently seen in

20              the, the investigation continued for quite a while.  The

21              advice given to my office by the District Attorney was

22              that they wanted you to sign this piece of paper, which

23              is entitled waiver which is really a statement of under-

24              standing of the Miranda warnings and not a waiver, that

25              they wanted us to do that because there were possible

26              criminal implications.  We didn't want to jeopardize

27              their case which we viewed much more important than ours.

28              A man's license is nothing compared to a felony charge

29              and we didn't want to in any way harm their case.  That's

30              why we did that.  I would ask why is it so important that

31              you know who this individual is, if there is one and I

32              believe there was an initial letter of some sort?

-16-

1 BIGLIERI: Well, there must be I think because you, I think alluded
2          to the point there that the Sheriff's Department and the
3          D. A. had contacted you so that confirms my earlier, my
4          suspicions.  Why, I'll tell you why because first of all
5          as an elected public official you won't do, get off on
6          the publicity and, but you don't have to stay there.  You
7          can quit any time you want, you don't have to run for the
8          job, but I sort of like the position I hold with the
9          city.  I'm very proud of the record that I have accom-
10         plished in the last five years but I don't think that
11         anyone has that right to start a complaint like this, or
12         initate an action based on absolutely no grounds whatso-
13         ever and this was true in this case.  This was a perfect-
14         ly legitimate real estate transaction between two people
15         and neither one of them have filed a complaint and the
16         organized crime unit which was funded with federal money
17         and has spent to this date, I'd say an excess of
18         $500,000, and coincidently the Grand Jury Report just
19         came out yesterday morning with no indictments against
20         anyone.  I think this a real totalitarian state.  What
21         we're
22 EDMONDSON: What, let me set the record straight.  We are not in
23          collusion and never have been.  Now, speaking for myself
24          personally and for the investigation that Marv Laqua
25          conducted to my knowledge, we are not in collusion,
26          assisting, acting as agents for or in any way connected
27          with the investigation with the Sheriff's Department.
28 BIGLIERI: Although,
29 EDMONDSON: We're not their agents.  We knew that they were investi-
30          gating, yes.  But, and that is where this thing came
31          from.  In other words, we did not want to hurt their
32          investigation in any way.  We were proceeding along our

-17-

73

1  EDMONDSON: own little route there.

2  BIGLIERI: I thought they were instructing you with their request.

3  EDMONDSON: Not at their request.

4  BIGLIERI: You mean on your own volition.

5  EDMONDSON: Wait a second.  I'm not going to be cross examined.

6  BIGLIERI: No, I'm not cross examining.  I'm merely say'in that, is

7  this standard procedure to walk in with a Miranda Deci-

8  sion and you talk to someone, a real estate broker.

9  EDMONDSON: I would say its going to be standard procedure and I

10  would advise that it be standard procedure any time there

11  is possible criminal indictments.  Yes.

12  BIGLIERI: Well, don't you think that this person being investigated

13  has a right then to know what you're really investigating

14  or looking for because the organized crime unit if you

15  are referring to them continuous, has, was in my office

16  prior to this and have a complete file.  A complete file,

17  as a matter of fact, its incorporated in the Grand Jury

18  Report as exhibits in the back of the report.  All the

19  real estate documents

20  EDMONDSON: But I don't see what bearing that has.  If anything that

21  cuts against what you are insinuating, that we are

22  colluding with the Sheriff.

23  BIGLIERI: Mr. Edmondson, I'm merely saying I just can't understand

24  why you would refuse for a two year period to let me

25  know who would initiated the action wherein your people

26  came into my office, and asked to see documents when they

27  already had the documents in their possession

28  EDMONDSON: Apparently

29  BIGLIERI: Or what they were looking for.  That's what I want to

30  know, what they were looking for that you could supply

31  them that they didn't have.

32  EDMONDSON: Now wait a second.  That's kind of a heavy assumption

-18-

74

1  EDMONDSON: that we're acting as their agents and I've just said that

2            the Real Estate Division never has and never will act as

3            the agent Sheriff's office. Why should they?

4  BIGLIERI: Well you just said

5  EDMONDSON: First off, they spent $500,000 on a huge staff to do all

6            this investigating. We're not trained, you know, speak-

7            ing for Marv and the investigators. We're not trained

8            as criminal investigators. That's not the idea. This

9            was a simple, potential violation of 645.

10  BIGLIERI: What was, what was simple violation?

11  EDMONDSON: What was being investigated.

12  BIGLIERI: Who said there was a violation?

13  EDMONDSON: I'm saying it was a potential violation. That's why

14            they were in there.

15  BIGLIERI: Then if anybody, like if I said in the letter, on the

16            phone with you two years ago, if I had twenty-five people

17            I thought were violating something and you said yes, we

18            would investigate them all. Strictly on my say so, that

19            I thought that there was an investigation, I mean thought

20            there was something wrong.

21  EDMONDSON: Well, I think there is a certain amount of inherent dis-

22            cretion, but if you read 610 strictly, or not 610, yes

23            610 the one I just read strictly. Yes, you would have to

24            say that any time someone complains against a real estate

25            broker has to be investigated. Wouldn't you want it in-

26            vestigated as a taxpayer. Wouldn't you want that thing

27            laid to rest. See when you have to look at it from the

28            standpoint

29  BIGLIERI: It all depends on where your at.

30  EDMONDSON: Well, I mean

31  BIGLIERI: In my case, I don't mind you investigating. I merely

32            again state my position that I don't know why after six

-19-

1 BIGLIERI: hundred days until just this minute, I didn't know where
2 the action came from which initiated your investigators
3 to call me and ask to see that file.
4 EDMONDSON: Do you now know?
5 BIGLIERI: Yes, because of what you're saying.
6 EDMONDSON: Where did it come from?
7 BIGLIERI: From you, from the Sheriff's Department and the District
8 Attorney. You said it and I imagine that it is on tape.
9 EDMONDSON: What I'm saying is that this document here which is en-
10 titled waiver, which you presented the Advisory Commis-
11 sion today which has your name on it and which you in-
12 dicated you refused to sign.
13 BIGLIERI: Right.
14 EDMONDSON: The idea for presenting that to you prior to having your
15 statement comes from the D. A. calling me, talking to
16 me and saying hey we're looking into this. Don't screw
17 up the case for us. Better give him the Miranda warn-
18 ings. There might be possible criminal indictments.
19 Period.
20 BIGLIERI: But on his actions you proceeded, or the investigators
21 did, to investigate
22 EDMONDSON: Yes, sure. I would, I'm proud of it. I'm glad I did it.
23 I'd do it again and again, again, again.
24 HASS: Well what the Real Estate, let me ask a question here.
25 Now we're getting into a situation where you're talking
26 about possible criminals here versus the right of a
27 privilege license.
28 EDMONDSON: Their case
29 HASS: And I don't, boy come in and hit me with something like
30 that, I'd kick somebody right out of my office.
31 EDMONDSON: Well, that's your right
32 HASS: Unless, I know, but for God's sake

-20-

```
 1  EDMONDSON:That's fine.
 2  HASS:      If you've got, if there's a criminal situation then let
 3             the D. A. do it.
 4  BIGLIERI: That's right.
 5  EDMONDSON:Well, I mean that's policy matter.  Angus should talk to
 6             that.
 7  HASS:      Listen
 8  KROLAK:    But what you're saying is that there still isn't anything
 9             in the file that indicates there was a complaint or
10             what the complaint was about.
11  BIGLIERI: Nobody will answer.  Nobody will tell me.
12  EDMONDSON:Wait a second now.  You've, there has never been any
13             publicity about the Real Estate Division case.  You've
14             never had a complaint filed against you.
15  BIGLIERI: That's right.
16  EDMONDSON:Right.
17  BIGLIERI: You know why there hasn't been any publicity because
18             there hasn't been any publicity in two years on my part.
19             There has been an awful lot of publicity.
20  EDMONDSON:And the Real Estate Division has gone to the papers
21             and said that they're investigating?
22  BIGLIERI: No, neither have I.  That's not your position to go to
23             the papers.
24  EDMONDSON:Exactly.
25  BIGLIERI: You would put yourself in one heck of a position.
26  EDMONDSON:Exactly.  There is no complaint against you right now.
27  BIGLIERI: Yes, there is because Mr. McLeod's letter said it's
28             still open.
29  EDMONDSON:Filed.  There is no filed.
30  BIGLIERI: It is still under investigation.  That's what he said.
31  EDMONDSON:That's right.  That's right.  It is an ongoing investiga-
32             tion.
```

-21-

1 BIGLIERI: Still open then.

2 EDMONDSON: That's right.

3 BIGLIERI: And when it is closed I will be notified.

4 HASS: Well, can these things keep on going on and on and
5 forever, Angus?

6 KROLAK: Why?

7 McLEOD: As long as there is something to be investigated, I
8 don't see why we couldn't.

9 HASS: Yea, but how long does it take to investigate something?

10 HANNAFIN: Read him the statute.

11 EDMONDSON: Yea, eventually you run into the three year statute of
12 limitations.

13 BIGLIERI: After it closes. But this hasn't closed yet.

14 EDMONDSON: No, after the act, and that's when it closes.

15 BIGLIERI: But it's still on.

16 EDMONDSON: After the act itself. Three years can be extended.

17 HASS: Well, that's a long time to keep somebody on the hook,
18 isn't it?

19 KROLAK: Yea, I mean you've notified somebody and for three years
20 you don't have to go back and tell them anything? You
21 can just keep an eye on him.

22 EDMONDSON: I think so.

23 KROLAK: It's kind of intimidation.

24 EDMONDSON: Wait, I don't understand. What's intimidating about it
25 when there is no complaint that has been filed?

26 HASS and KROLAK: Then why haven't they closed the case.

27 KROLAK: Why have an open case then?

28 SCHULTZ: There's no formal. Why is the case open if there is no
29 complaint filed?

30 EDMONDSON: Wait a second, wait a second, we're mixing apples and
31 oranges. What I mean by complaint is that complaint,
32 that document signed by the Administrator which goes to

-22-

1 EDMONDSON: the licensee which says you are on notice that on such

2 and such a day we're going to discuss the following items

3 alleging wrong doing and you may lose your license or

4 may have it suspended. That is the complaint. There

5 may be a complaining letter from an injured party or an

6 involved party which may have started this, I don't

7 really remember. I believe there was some letter of

8 some sort. Okay, the point is, no complaint formally

9 has been filed against you in front of this body which

10 acts as an administrative hearing body. There has been

11 no complaint filed. I don't think that you have a right

12 to foreclose an investigation until it is through.

13 Again, I think your position as a public officer you

14 must be confronted with this regularly where you know

15 things that are going on that have to be thoroughly

16 looked at and by george it takes a long time because you

17 don't have enough money or adequate resources.

18 BIGLIERI: That's not true, Mr.

19 HASS: Well, I was thinking here as a public officer and with

20 the District Attorney investigating this case, if there

21 is an indictment, and if there is a conviction, then we

22 can take action under the 645.

23 EDMONDSON: I don't think that we're bound by law to wait on anybody

24 be it the D. A. or the Federal Attorney or whatever. It

25 maybe, again, this runs into policy. I don't set the

26 policy. Maybe if I'd been doing it, I would have waited

27 until it was all over and then do the Real Estate Divi-

28 sion's bit. Anyway at that point and time it was decided

29 that the Real Estate investigation would be concurrent

30 with the one being conducted by the, whoever was doing

31 it up there in Washoe County. I see nothing illegal

32 about that or wrong about that. If anything, it brings

-23-

```
1  EDMONDSON: it to a close more quickly.  And also nonindictable
2             offenses could be offenses under 645.  You could lose
3             your license for, your license for something that
4             wouldn't be a criminal violation.  That's true, so I
5             mean, I see nothing illegal about what happened.
6  HASS:      It smacks of a witch hunt.
7  HAMMOND:   I mean it's more prescription than anything else.
8  HASS:      Mr. Lewis.
9  LEWIS:     Yes, two things here that are bothering me.  Mr.
10            Edmondson seems to indicate that the Administrator can
11            investigate anything that he wants to.
12 EDMONDSON: Right.
13 LEWIS:     As I'm reading 645.610 here it says:  investigation of
14            actions of licensees and other persons.  The Administra-
15            tor may upon his own motion and shall upon the complaint
16            in writing of any person investigate the actions.  It
17            has been in this particular case they had apparently or
18            if there is no written complaint because there is indi-
19            cate in the things that there is no written complaint
20            and then Mr. Edmondson also stated further back that it
21            was the duty of the Administrator's office to go ahead
22 —          and do their own investigation but back in 645.190, it
23            very clearly stipulates that yes they should go ahead
24            and do their investigation but their investigation pro-
25            cedures are to be published and there can be set up and
26            approved by the, by this Commission.  There seems to be
27.           no such regulations set up and approved by this Commis-
28            sion that would authorize them to proceed in the manner
29            they did in Mr. Biglieri's case.
30 HASS:      Is this an isolated case?
31 LEWIS:     These are the things that we're
32 HASS:      Let me ask this.  Is this an isolated situation regarding
```

-24-

80

```
1  HASS:      Mr. Biglieri or are there other cases in the Reno
2  HAMMOND:   That is the one that has generated the question and what
3             comes out here is.  You use the term isolated.  Mr.
4             Biglieri is a member of the Reno Board of REALTORS and
5             therefore, he is treated like the other 537 members and
6             if Mr. Biglieri could be under this same type of pre-
7             scription, would the other 537 be so.
8  EDMONDSON: Do you know of any other specific cases?
9  HAMMOND:   I don't think that is germane.
10 EDMONDSON: I'm asking a question.
11 HAMMOND:   No.  I don't
12 SCHULTZ:   Do you know of any
13 HAMMOND:   Specific
14 LEWIS:     There have been indications, yes.
15 HASS   :   Mr. Myers.  Bill Myers
16 MYERS:     Yes, this all started when I was President of the board
17            last year and I, the intent here was not to come down
18            and argue or try to argue a point or anything.  The intent
19            was just simply to find out what procedure would be from
20            here on in so that we would know which way to go.  The
21            second thing that I would like to say, I am on the Board
22            of Directors of the State Association, and I don't ever
23            remember our board even discussing it.  The State Board
24 McLEOD:    I didn't say the board was discussing it.  I said I talked
25            with Argeres and he said as far as he is concerned, this
26            is an effort solely by the Reno Board and it is not
27            supported by the State Association.
28 KROLAK:    We think that is rather irrelevant.  I think anyone, any
29            licensee has the privilege of coming in whether he wants
30            to be represented by a group or by himself, and I think
31            that is not really important as to who generated it.
32            Which department of REALTORS generated it?
```

-25-

81

1  EDMONDSON: One other thing I would like to set straight is there

2  has been some discussion here that we're 510 days over

3  the ninety day ruling. Statute specifically provides

4  that ninety days from the filing of a formal complaint

5  a hearing must be held. There is, has been no formal

6  complaint. That's a term of art that means the document

7  which I described to you earlier. It is something that

8  comes to you with notice on it, and this is part of, you

9  know, the trend to have speedy hearings. So there has

10  been no document like that so as far as I'm concerned

11  legally we're not 510 days beyond the point where we

12  can deal with this. There is a three year statute of

13  limitations. Three years from that incident the Real

14  Estate Division no longer is . . . One other thing, I

15  think I should speak for Angus and on behalf here as far,

16  I think I heard you correctly you were insinuating that

17  the Real Estate Division might have had something to do

18  with the current release of the Grand Jury Report or in

19  some way with the Grand Jury Report.

20  BIGLIERI: No, I said that I thought I've suspicioned all along

21  that this was part of that ongoing investigation and

22  you've confirmed it by telling me that the District

23  Attorney

24  EDMONDSON: No, I've not confirmed that

25  BIGLIERI: Well you did. It's on tape.

26  EDMONDSON: Okay, we're not

27  BIGLIERI: District Attorney asked you to check this out or to

28  investigate it.

29  EDMONDSON: We can listen to it over and over again and I don't think

30  that you're going to understand what I'm saying. But go

31  ahead

32  BIGLIERI: I think I will. I have the proof. It is on your table.

1  BIGLIERI: There has got to be a specific case number there because
2           it spells one out. There is a case number.
3  EDMONDSON: There is a case number.
4  BIGLIERI: And it is still open, ongoing. I'd like to know when
5           it is going to be terminated.
6  SCHULTZ: Bob I'd like to know when, if a case number has been
7           filed, if that doesn't take a formal complaint in order
8           to do that.
9  EDMONDSON: Okay. The way these are handled is, the way they have
10           always been handled. When the cases are initiated they
11           are either assigned a number or a name of some sort.
12           From that point on you refer to that particular file or
13           that set of papers. That's it. Many, many, many com-
14           plaints, or complaints from injured parties. I'm saying
15           now, are not acted on nor would you want them to be acted
16           on. In other words, internally the Real Estate Division
17           determines that these things aren't worthy of continuing.
18  SCHULTZ: Bob, do you think that 600 days is an undue amount of
19           time it would take to decide that this is something that
20           we don't want to act on?
21  EDMONDSON: Well, the Grand Jury itself has taken over 600 days. I
22           suppose you could look at it that way.
23  SCHULTZ: Yea, but they are investigating a criminal complaint.
24           We're investigating something that may be relative to
25           that at this particular point, but I think frankly, if
26           we haven't got anything any more supportive than the
27           decision of a District Attorney to have a waiver or
28           Miranda Decision put before the, a licensee and the fact
29           that this might have some potential law violation, I
30           believe we ought to be a little bit more forthright with
31           our licensees to me. I don't think we are a police
32           state, we're a regulatory body. That's been my opinion

-27-

| | |
|---|---|
| 1 | SCHULTZ: all along. If we have to have a bunch of policemen to |
| 2 | go around and see to it that the licensees dot all their |
| 3 | i's and cross all their t's and don't deal with only the |
| 4 | people that have white shirts, not the ones who wear |
| 5 | blue shirts, speaking of the underworld side in the day- |
| 6 | light side if you want to go into this particular situa- |
| 7 | tion, then I believe that we had better change our entire |
| 8 | law. We better change our entire rules and regulations. |
| 9 | And you know what else, I'm going to retire from the |
| 10 | real estate business if that's the way it's going to be |
| 11 | conducted. I think we are a group of professionals. I |
| 12 | believe we should stay a group of professionals, or at |
| 13 | least try to get to be more professional in our activi- |
| 14 | ties and I think the Division is very professional in |
| 15 | most of its dealings. In this particular case, I think |
| 16 | maybe they've had some extraneous pressures. That there |
| 17 | have been outside pressures, and I believe that I think |
| 18 | that we had better reassess this regulatory and law |
| 19 | enforcement angle. |
| 20 | EDMONDSON:To respond to that, although I don't think I really have |
| 21 | to, the broad generalizations being bandied about that |
| 22 | Angus is running a Gestapo shop here and I don't think |
| 23 | we've seen anything that is anything like that in it. |
| 24 | The charge here we've got a man who feels under great |
| 25 | pressure. He's in public office. He feels probably |
| 26 | harassed and he wants to know when a certain investiga- |
| 27 | tion is going to be completed. The legislature tells |
| 28 | him that three years from the date of the offense is that |
| 29 | time after which nothing more can happen and is really |
| 30 | that time at which the investigation has to terminate by |
| 31 | law. The legislature set the three years. |
| 32 | KROLAK: But there is nothing that says you have to divulge what |

-28-

84

```
 1  KROLAK:    the offense was.  Don't they?
 2  HASS:      Who the complainant
 3  SILVAGNI:  Until a complaint is filed.
 4  EDMONDSON:Again, there is no complaint filed here.  We are talking
 5             kind of rumor upon hearsay because there is nothing
 6  SILVAGNI:  In other words, you don't have to report an investigation
 7  EDMONDSON:No.
 8  SILVAGNI:  That's the whole
 9  HASS:      I think the Commission has been remiss as far as comply-
10             ing with NRS 645.195 because it states that the Commis-
11             sion shall adopt rules and regulations with respect to
12             such investigations.  It doesn't say may, it says shall.
13             So I would suggest that the Division come up with some
14             rules and regulations regarding their investigative
15             procedures subject to public hearings.
16  KROLAK:    That's what you want
17  HASS:      When do you think that can be done, Angus?
18  McLEOD:    We'll take it under advisement here, Bob.
19  EDMONDSON:One other section I think I should refer you to before
20             we get off this
21  HASS:      Under advisement?
22  KROLAK:    Does that mean you'll do it?
23  HASS:      It says shall, Angus, we're trying to comply with the
24             law too.  It says shall, it doesn't say may.
25  KROLAK:    I think it has to
26  HASS:      Now either if you don't, then of course we'll end up
27             doing it.  I think you could have something
28  SCHULTZ:   I'd like to take issue with Bob's remark that if any
29             implications are running around that Angus is running a
30             Gestapo shop.  I don't think that is the implication.  I
31             think that Angus has inherited a situation here, and is
32             trying to make the best of it under the existing condi-
```

-29-

85

| | | |
|---|---|---|
| 1 | SCHULTZ: | tions. I don't think that the inference that even I |
| 2 | | might have implied that is correct, and I hope that |
| 3 | | Angus understands that. But I simply feel that if Angus |
| 4 | | was under this particular type of pressure as Clyde has |
| 5 | | been for this particular length of time under something |
| 6 | | which has now been proven that there probably-is no |
| 7 | | justification. I'm going to make that assumption. It's |
| 8 | | just an assumption. |
| 9 | EDMONDSON: | Fred, actually, I really would rather |
| 10 | SCHULTZ: | Well, |
| 11 | EDMONDSON: | you wouldn't say any more because you are the hearing |
| 12 | | body. The case is still open. |
| 13 | SCHULTZ: | We're just trying to gather information I thought at |
| 14 | | this point. |
| 15 | KROLAK: | I think that the point that they would like to get |
| 16 | | across is just what Bob pointed out. That there should |
| 17 | | be some guide for the investigations and that the Commis- |
| 18 | | sion obviously is to establish some rules. |
| 19 | HASS: | It doesn't say maybe |
| 20 | KROLAK: | In cooperation with the Division we can do this. |
| 21 | BARNES: | That's for inspection of records Bob, not investigations. |
| 22 | McLEOD: | Inspection of records |
| 23 | HANNAFIN: | It doesn't say investigations |
| 24 | HASS: | Wait a minute. |
| 25 | SILVAGNI: | The Division with brokers records |
| 26 | HANNAFIN: | Inspection. |
| 27 | SILVAGNI: | That they were investigating his records of the trans- |
| 28 | | action. |
| 29 | HASS: | To such inspection. Division to inspect brokers records, |
| 30 | | rules and regulations for inspection. The Real Estate |
| 31 | | Division shall regularly inspect the records of all real |
| 32 | | estate brokers and insure compliance with the provisions |

-30-

86

1  HASS:        of this chapter.  The Commission shall adopt rules and
2               regulations with respect to such inspections.  What are
3               you inspecting?  You're inspecting records.  What did
4               you expect to get from Clyde Biglieri except in records?
5  SILVAGNI:    In transaction
6  McLEOD:      If you don't get all the records, then what are you
7               going to do then?
8  HASS:        Well, then I guess that leaves an area that would be
9               subject to your determination.
10 McLEOD:      We'll have something on this topic for you.
11 HASS:        Yea, I'm not, like I say, I'm not blaming you.  I think
12              just like Fred, that you inherited a situation.
13 LEWIS:       Can I make one comment in relation to Clyde's situation.
14              Under 645.620, it says the Real Estate Division shall
15              maintain in its office a public document or other
16              record which indicates public document or another public
17              record from time to time can read on for these investiga-
18              tions
19 EDMONDSON:   You can go see that if you want.  There is one.    *NO.*
20 LEWIS:       So I feel and this is from listening to this.  The situ-
21              ation where they say its confidential and the client
22              isn't allowed to know what the charges are or, there
23              certainly ought to be as Fred indicated, some document
24              that instigated this investigation within that file,
25              which nobody seems to have ever produced.
26 EDMONDSON:   The public docket is    *Not True*
27 LEWIS:       Yet it ought to be, there ought to be a public file on
28              record concerning this case, but there doesn't seem to
29              be one.
30 EDMONDSON:   If you want to see a public docket.  There is one.
31              There's a public docket on all complaints and all deci-
32              sions.

-31-

1 LEWIS:       Then why would they write to Clyde and tell him it is

2                confidential, he couldn't see it.

3 EDMONDSON: Because there is no formal complaint.

4 SILVAGNI:  No complaint.  No complaint has ever been filed.

5 EDMONDSON: There's no complaint that's been filed with this man.

6                There's no notice of a hearing that he's received.  I

7                think that this is kind of a strange procedure where the

8                person that is being investigated determines the form

9                and extent and nature of the investigation.  I don't

10               think that you gentlemen would want that.  If you think

11               about it from the other end of it, I'm not saying that

12               Mr. Biglieri has done anything at all.  I'm just saying

13               that the form of the investigation has got to be deter-

14               mined by the investigator not the man being investigated.

15 HAMMOND:   May I ask my original question again of 10, December?

16               Specifically, what is the practice past, present and

17               most importantly proposed as to informing a potential

18               respondent as to the exact nature of the complaints and

19               the identity of the complainants during the informal

20               phase implied in Section VIII of aforesaid rules and

21          .    regulations.  That's basically the question, and if I

22               am to infer from your replies to that, Mr. Edmondson,

23               that there is no, there isn't now, hasn't been in the

24               past and is not proposed in the future to be any method

25               of informing a potential respondent during the informal

26               phase.  In other words, the informal phase can be a

27               gossip phase right up until the expiration of the thirty

28          —    six months.  Is that a correct inference on my part?

29 EDMONDSON: Well, you know what my answer is going to be.  Let me

30               say this.

31 HAMMOND:   If I had of, I wouldn't have asked it.

32 EDMONDSON: Right.  That is incorrect and I would say this that in-

1  EDMONDSON: vestigations take the course of, just exactly as you

2  would imagine, in other words, people go out and ask

3  questions. Investigators do not go out and libel people.

4  Alright they can't do that. We know that because they

5  are exceeding their authority etc., etc. So we know

6  what investigations are. Investigations are a bunch of

7  people going around asking questions and saying hey do

8  you know X, Y, Z or you have got some documents that show

9  X, Y, Z. That's what they are. That's what they have

10  always been, that's what they always will be. So I don't

11  think there is any, I don't think there is a real lack

12  of understanding here, and I don't think that inherently

13  there is any right, at least as far as I can find in the

14  statute, that every single fact has to be shown to the

15  licensee. As you know, cross examination often you use

16  facts that you know, that he doesn't know you know and

17  bounce them back and forth to determine whether someone

18  is telling the truth. And I think that is fine. That's

19  what investigation about. Again, we're not public. At

20  this point nothing has been out in the papers, there is

21  no formal hearing, there are no charges right now. To

22  me it is just a normal investigation that's running its

23  course. Maybe it's taking too long.

24  HASS:      Don't you have various types of investigation. One would

25  be just kind of dropping into the office and say looking

26  at the trust account. There is no complaint.

27  SILVAGNI: Record inspection

28  HASS:      There is a record inspection type of thing and then of

29  course when you have a, looking into a specific trans-

30  action then you would be subject to a specific complaint.

31  I would think, wouldn't it?

32  EDMONDSON: Wouldn't have to. You mean a

-33-

89

1 | HASS: | Well, somebody, in other words, its either administr,
2 | | its either initiated by the Administrator or the Divi-
3 | | sion, or by a complainant in a complaint about specific
4 | | actions.
5 | EDMONDSON:That's right.
6 | LEWIS: | It seems that in consideration in setting up the rules
7 | | and regulations, there's gotta be some provision in there
8 | | that where the investigator should be required at least
9 | | to give the investigatee an indication as to what it is
10 | | he is being investigated for, even if he doesn't come
11 | | forth with any formal charge or complaint but just the
12 | | nature, the reason why they are looking into his records.
13 | | If they're looking in with, into his records for any
14 | | other purpose then purely administrative.
15 | HASS: | I think, I think really that's probably why that one
16 | | sentence was in 645.95 is that, to establish some rules
17 | | and regulations which have not been done and, so I think
18 | | that once these are considered in a public hearing, and
19 | | give them a chance to look them over and put some inputs
20 | | into and it will be a guideline for all of us to work
21 | | with.
22 | SILVAGNI: | The policy for investigations
23 | HASS: | Well, with this I'm suggesting that the Division go over
24 | | it because this is the pervue. If there is no further
25 | | comment, we'll call this hearing closed, and we'll have
26 | | about a ten minute recess.
27 | BIGLIERI: | Mr. Chairman, I'd like to request a transcript of this
28 | | and I will be willing to pay for it and a fee to tran-
29 | | scribe it. Please have your staff transcribe it and
30 | | send a copy of it.
31 | EDMONDSON:Ask Angus.
32 | ----------

-34-

90

1 | McLEOD:    Sure, we'll get one for him.

2 | BIGLIERI: Thank you very much for your time.   I appreciate that.

3 | HASS:    Thank you Mr. Biglieri.

1    I, Kathy Noland, employed by the Real Estate Division,
2 prepared this transcript from a tape recording of the Nevada Real
3 Estate Advisory Commission meeting, Real Estate Division office,
4 Nye Building, 201 South Fall Street, Room No. 125, Carson City,
5 Nevada, on March 16, 1976.

6
7                              _Kathy Noland_
8                              Kathy Noland
9
10
11
12
13
14
15
16
17
18
19
20
21
22
23
24
25
26
27
28
29
30
31
32

-36-

The point of the hearing was to try and define the scope of investigations by investigators for the Real Estate Division and what information those individuals being investigated had prior to a formal complaint being filed.

It was during the course of this hearing that my case came up, that I had been approached by Nevada Real Estate Division investigators who didn't have a formal complaint or even a case number, who wanted me to sign a Miranda warning but refused to give me any information. Tom Lewis, the president of the Reno Board of REALTORS stated in the minutes from that 1976 Nevada Real Estate Advisory Commission meeting that I "wasn't satisfied with his contact with the investigators and the manner in which they approached his office and tried to get answers and couldn't seem to."

It was during this hearing that counsel for the commission, Bob Edmondson, stated that Nevada Revised Statute 645.610 gave the administrator the authority to investigate on his own with or without any complaint to start with. He went on to add that at the same time the investigation was underway, the Washoe County Sheriff's Office was investigating the land transaction between Conforte and the Convention Authority and that the investigators for the Real Estate Division were advised by the District Attorney's office to have me and my salesman sign the Miranda warning because the investigation held possible criminal implications.

"We didn't want to jeopardize their case, which we viewed much more important than ours," Edmondson stated in the record of the proceedings, and went on to say the Miranda warning was presented to me because: "The idea for presenting that to you prior to having your statement comes from the D.A. calling me, talking to me and saying, 'Hey, we're looking into this. Don't screw up the case for us. Better give him the Miranda warning. There might be possible criminal indictments.' Period."

At this point the hearing broke down for a while, turning into a shouting match. But here are a few facts to ponder:

March 29, 1973, Robert Rusk, chairman, and Frank Freeman, director, filed a Notice of Intent from Washoe County to apply to Law Enforcement Assistance Administration for a $185,520 Organized Crime Prevention Program grant.

April 16, 1974, Gordon L. Foote, chairman, and Frank Freeman, director, filed a Notice of Intent from Washoe County to apply to Law Enforcement Assistance Administration for a $249,324 Organized Crime Unit Operational Grant, with $28,024 in county money and $277,348 federal. The grant followed a decision in April 1973 when the Area Council of Governments met and determined to initiate a county-wide organized crime unit to undertake the discovery, investigation and evaluation of organized crime within Washoe County and peripheral areas. The proposed project request was to cover second-year funding of an existing grant program.

The goals of the Organized Crime Unit included discovering organized crime activities through investigation; educating and informing the community in a continuing program aimed at stopping organized crime; training law enforcement personnel to give them what they needed for the program; and increasing the likelihood of successful prosecutions against organized crime targets.

Apparently the Council received the grant, because there are Discretionary Grant Progress Reports filed October 21,

1975, to the U.S. Department of Justice, Law Enforcement Assistance Administration from Nevada Commission on Crime, Delinquency and Corrections. The implementing sub-grantee is listed as the Washoe County Sheriff's Department for the County-Wide Organized Crime Unit and the report shows a grant amount of $249,324 for the period of July 1 through September 15, 1975. Another Discretionary Grant Progress Report filed in April 1976 shows a grant amount of $197,651.

While the Discretionary Grant Reports indicate the Organized Crime Unit was looking at activities as diverse as narcotics violations and carnival game rip-offs, it is likely the specter of prostitution, in the form of Joe Conforte, would have lured them. This is probably fair.

The Sheriff's Office, having put together an Organized Crime Unit, would naturally go looking for organized crime, and prostitution was a crime within Washoe County, which had never legalized prostitution. Mustang Ranch and Joe Conforte were right next door in Storey County, less than a 20-minute drive from downtown Reno. Conforte was an attractive target for law enforcement agencies. Yet, he wasn't doing anything illegal.

Conforte bought land from the Capurros in Reno and turned around and sold it at a loss to the Convention Authority. He hoped to make money by selling the land adjacent to that parcel and instead wound up losing it during his much-publicized battles with the IRS.

In the meantime, the Organized Crime Unit and the Washoe County District Attorney's office were interested in the land sale from Capurro to Conforte and from Conforte to the Convention Authority. If a few innocent people got pulled into the investigation, it seemed that the opinion of those involved was that attempting to combat organized crime outweighed the damage done to a few lives and reputations.

I wasn't the only local politician dragged into the Conforte net and not the only City Councilman to appear before the grand jury. I wasn't the only one the papers urged to resign from my post. I was just the one who fought back.

I continue to fight back, 30 years later, despite the obstacles along the way, the fact that the newspaper continued to bask in the glory of a Pulitzer Prize won for journalistic reporting that knowingly failed to ever address the facts or redress the injuries: I did nothing wrong. No individual, newspaper syndicate or governmental agency has ever apologized.

This is my side of the story — the side that has not been told. The truth.

# APPENDIX A

**[Pages 100-147] Grand Jury Report**
Tuesday, March 16, 1976, the *Nevada State Journal* (then owned by Reno Newspapers, Inc.) printed the grand jury report investigating the Capurro-Conforte-RSCVA land transaction in its entirety, despite the fact that several of the individuals mentioned in the report were never indicted for any kind of criminal activity. My life changed when the grand jury report was filed and the 237 newspaper articles that followed began to appear.

TABLE OF CONTENTS

appendix a

# TABLE OF CONTENTS

Page 2

# P R E F A C E

The law of the State of Nevada provides:

"1.  The Grand Jury must inquire into . . . the misconduct in office of public officers of every description within the county.

"2.  The Grand Jury may inquire into and report on any and all matters affecting the morals, health and general welfare of the inhabitants of the county, or of any administrative division thereof, or of any township, incorporated city, irrigation district or town therein." ***

NRS 172.175.

Pursuant to the legal responsibility vested in the Grand Jury, this Jury began its investigation of the matters contained within this report in July, 1974. At the outset, the Grand Jury investigation focused upon what is commonly referred to as the Conforte Land Transaction wherein brothel owner Joe Conforte purchased approximately three hundred forty four (344) acres of property from a Sparks ranching family, and thereafter sold a portion of the property to the Convention Authority. The Grand Jury's investigation also centered upon Sparks City Government as it existed prior to the Spring elections of 1975, and upon the activities of certain members of the then Sparks City Council.

The scope of the Grand Jury's investigation broadened considerably as evidence relevant to one facet of the investigation led to new areas where additional inquiry appeared

1   warranted.  As will be seen in this report, by the time that the

2   investigation was concluded, it reached not only into the

3   Sparks City Council but also to a degree into the Reno City

4   Council and the Washoe County Commission.  Other public entities,

5   former public officials, and current public officials also fell

6   under the purview of the Grand Jury.

7          The Grand Jury is not issuing any criminal charges.

8   No crimes have been shown from the evidence discussed in this

9   report and the Grand Jury stresses that nothing said in this

10  report is intended to accuse, imply, or create an innuendo that

11  any person has committed a criminal offense.  Because no criminal

12  charges are being issued, the Grand Jury has elected to release

13  what it considers to be an in depth report of the major areas

14  in which investigation and review were undertaken and in which

15  comment can be made.

16         Pursuant to Nevada law, the Grand Jury can report on

17  conduct which does not constitute the commission of a crime and

18  which is relevant to the health, safety and welfare of the

19  citizens of Washoe County.  Not only does the Grand Jury have

20  the jurisdiction to report on such conduct, but the members of

21  this Grand Jury also believe they have an absolute obligation to

22  report their findings in this particular investigation.  This

23  report represents the Grand Jury's effort in this regard and is

24  supported by the concurrence of each and every member of the

25  Grand Jury, no Grand Juror dissenting as to any part of this

26  report.

27         Because of the length of this report and the scope

28  of the Grand Jury's investigation, it is the recommendation of

the Grand Jurors that readers of this report carefully read it
in its entirety and consider the inter-relationship of each part
of the report with the other.  Conduct reported in one portion
may not in itself seem particularly significant; however, the
Grand Jurors believe that in the context of the entire report,
everything contained herein is indeed relevant to an enlightened
understanding of the Grand Jury's investigation.

The Grand Jurors believe that this investigation, this
report, and other official action resulting from the investigation have been most important to the public interest and welfare
of the citizens of Reno, Sparks and Washoe County.  Because of
the scope of the investigation and what the Grand Jury considers
to be the importance of its findings, the Jury has ordered copies
of this report prepared for release to any interested members
of the public.  Copies can be obtained at either the Washoe
County Clerk's Office or the Washoe County District Attorney's
Office, both offices located in the Courthouse in downtown Reno.
The Grand Jury is also having copies mailed to all elected
officials within this community.

## THE CAPURRO-CONFORTE LAND SALE

### I.
### BACKGROUND

John Brooke, City Manager of the City of Sparks from July 1967 to July of 1973, appeared before the Grand Jury and testified that by 1967 officials of the City of Sparks recognized the fact that a flood control dam was needed in the City of Sparks in the area of the Capurro-Gault property located near Sullivan Lane and Wedekind Road. This dam was necessary in order to capture flood waters coming from Sun Valley. The Capurro-Gault property was the only natural place for such a dam. As a result of the City's interest in the land, Brooke contacted the Capurros to explore the possibility of the City of Sparks purchasing the land for flood control.

During 1971, Sparks Mayor James Lillard indicated an interest in pursuing the matter as a joint recreation project along with flood control. After discussing it with the Mayor, Brooke was in contact with the Capurro family and actual negotiations were begun.

### II.
### THE CAPURRO-GAULT SALE TO CONFORTE

James E. Smith, realtor, testified before the Washoe County Grand Jury that in approximately September of 1972, he became interested in the Capurro-Gault land as a potential real estate prospect. Mr. Smith had previously sold Joe Conforte approximately two acres of land adjoining Conforte's Sullivan

-1-

103

1 Lane property and considered Joe Conforte to be a logical
2 purchaser of the Capurro-Gault land because Conforte lived near
3 the Capurro-Gault land, was believed by Smith to have money,
4 and had on the occasion of the prior sale handled by Smith,
5 expressed an interest in the land in the vicinity of his
6 residence.

7         At approximately the same time, in October of 1972,
8 James Smith spoke to Mr. and Mrs. John Capurro and their son
9 Wayne Capurro, an attorney at law, who acted as spokesman for
10 the Capurro-Gault family regarding the land. Smith requested
11 that he be given an exclusive real estate listing on the
12 approximately three hundred forty four (344) acres located in
13 the vicinity of Sullivan Lane and Wedekind Road. The Capurros
14 would not give Smith an exclusive real estate listing, but did
15 assure him that the family would listen to any bona fide offer
16 to purchase that Smith might present.

17         Mr. Smith, shortly thereafter, approached Joe Conforte
18 and suggested that Conforte buy the land. Conforte was not
19 interested in the land at that time and Smith abandoned his
20 efforts to persuade Conforte to purchase the Capurro-Gault land.

21         In late October or early November 1972, Smith received
22 a phone call from Joe Conforte asking him to come to Conforte's
23 house. When Smith arrived at Conforte's, Conforte said that he
24 had reconsidered the Capurro property. Conforte said he thought
25 he had a way of putting it together and he told Mr. Smith that
26 he had it figured out so that he would buy the land and the
27 City of Sparks and the Fair and Recreation Board (Convention
28 Authority) would build a golf course. Conforte stated that he

-2-

would end up with about one hundred (100) acres.  Conforte said,

> "If I get it at the right price, my
> acreage will go up to about maybe Twenty
> Five Thousand Dollars ($25,000.00) to
> Thirty Thousand Dollars ($30,000.00) an
> acre and I'll make myself a million dollars."

Thereafter Smith began negotiating with the Capurros and Gault on Conforte's behalf.  At the same time, representatives of the City of Sparks continued their discussions with the Capurros and Gault about the possibility of buying their land.

In February of 1973, prior to the sale of the land to Conforte, Sparks Councilman Gordon Foote made a motion that the Sparks City Council go on record as being in favor of buying the Capurro-Gault land.  Sparks Councilman Vernon and Sparks Councilman Lemberes voted against the City making a commitment to buy the land at that time without voter approval.  Shortly thereafter, the Council learned that Conforte had purchased the Capurro-Gault property.

On March 1, 1973, a deposit agreement was signed by Conforte.  (Exhibit No. 1)  By June 7, 1973, escrow instructions replaced other preliminary documents and the sale was concluded shortly thereafter.

Approximately three hundred forty four (344) acres were sold to Conforte at Five Thousand Dollars ($5,000.00) an acre for a total purchase price of One Million Seven Hundred Twenty Two Thousand Twenty Five Dollars ($1,722,025.00).  Also, Twenty Two Thousand Six Hundred Thirty Two Dollars ($22,632.00) was paid by Conforte for water rights.  The Capurro family agreed to pay a 5 percent commission in connection with the sale, which commission was in the approximate amount of

Eighty Six Thousand Dollars ($86,000.00). (Exhibit No. 2)

Mr. James Smith, an associate of Councilman Clyde Biglieri and his real estate company, Washoe Realty, agreed to a 5 percent real estate commission without the approval or knowledge of Washoe Realty or its owner, Reno City Councilman Biglieri. When Biglieri was informed that Smith had agreed to accept a 5 percent commission, he objected to the commission as not being the full and customary amount. Mr. Biglieri particularly objected when he was informed that he, Washoe Realty, and James Smith would only receive Forty Thousand Dollars ($40,000.00) of the Eighty Six Thousand Dollars ($86,000.00) commission, less than one-half of the 5 percent commission to be paid by the Capurros and Gault.

Smith had been informed by Conforte that there would be no deal unless they, Councilman Biglieri and James Smith, agreed to certain payments later set forth in a Letter of Instructions to First Commercial Title, Inc., dated June 5, 1973. (Exhibit No. 3) Those payments were to be made out of the 5 percent real estate commission to be paid by the Sellers, Capurro and Gault.

Although Biglieri objected to the commission being smaller than usual and being split as demanded by Conforte, upon realizing that the deal would not go through unless payments were made as set forth in the June 5, 1973, Letter of Instructions, Councilman Biglieri and James Smith agreed to accept the commission and go along with the payments detailed in the Letter of Instructions.

-4-

appendix a

1    Reno City Councilman Biglieri testified before the
2  Grand Jury that he told James Smith that he thought the commis-
3  sion should be split between himself and James Smith because
4  Smith had not consulted him and obtained his approval before
5  agreeing to accept a commission that was less than the customary
6  amount obtained at Washoe Realty.  Thus, after Smith agreed, he
7  received Twenty Thousand Dollars ($20,000.00) and Councilman
8  Biglieri received Twenty Thousand Dollars ($20,000.00).
9    The Letter of Instructions of June 5, 1973, (Exhibit
10  No. 3) was executed by Wayne Capurro, attorney for the Sellers,
11  and Stanley H. Brown, attorney for Joe Conforte, the Purchaser.
12  That Letter of Instructions divided the 5 percent commission to
13  be paid by the Capurros and Gault and pursuant to that Letter
14  of Instructions, checks were subsequently issued in the amounts
15  of Ten Thousand Five Hundred Dollars ($10,500.00) to S.E.&A.
16  Engineers and Planners, (Exhibit No. 4); Forty Thousand Dollars
17  ($40,000.00) to Washoe Realty, (Exhibit No. 5); Twenty Thousand
18  Dollars ($20,000.00) to Humphreys Real Estate, (Exhibit No. 6);
19  and Sixteen Thousand One Hundred One Dollars and twenty-five
20  cents ($16,101.25) to Joe Conforte, the Purchaser, (Exhibit
21  No. 7).
22    Nowhere in the agreements, documents of title, escrow
23  instructions, and other documents on file in connection with the
24  land transaction was there any mention of the fact that former
25  State Senator Stanley Drakulich was a real estate broker or
26  salesman with an interest in this transaction, or that he was
27  otherwise involved in the Capurro-Gault land transaction with
28  Conforte.  However, former Senator Stanley Drakulich received

107

Eighteen Thousand Dollars ($18,000.00) through William Humphreys, real estate broker. (Exhibit No. 8)  The check payable to Mr. Drakulich was dated June 7, 1973.  During the same month, Mr. Drakulich paid Eighteen Thousand One Hundred Seventy Dollars and fifty-three cents ($18,170.53) in back taxes and interest resulting from a criminal prosecution for failure to file a Federal income tax return.

The fact that former Senator Drakulich received Eighteen Thousand Dollars ($18,000.00) through William Humphreys was first made public on May 2, 1974, when the local newspapers published that fact.  (Exhibit No. 9)

Upon appearing before the Grand Jury, Mr. Drakulich complained that a copy of the $18,000.00 check had been provided to the newspapers by Sheriff Robert Galli.  Drakulich insisted that the Grand Jury determine whether or not Galli had so informed the press.  Sheriff Galli was called before the Grand Jury and testified that he did provide the information to the press.

William Humphreys, realtor, testified that he handled the Conforte transaction as a favor to Drakulich.  Humphreys testified that Drakulich asked him to receive the money and that he, Humphreys, received Two Thousand Dollars ($2,000.00) for this favor.  Humphreys testified that he knew of nothing that Drakulich did to earn the Eighteen Thousand Dollars ($18,000.00).  Also, Humphreys testified that he did nothing himself other than meet Joe Conforte at Drakulich's request.  None of the other witnesses who appeared were aware of anything that Drakulich had done to earn the commission.

1       Mr. Drakulich testified before the Grand Jury that he
2 heard that there was a land sale transaction taking place and
3 he approached Joe Conforte and asked Conforte if he could have
4 a commission in connection with the transaction. Conforte
5 agreed and although Drakulich was not a party to the land sale
6 negotiations which took place between Wayne Capurro, attorney
7 for Sellers, James Smith, Clyde Biglieri, and Stanley Brown,
8 attorney for Conforte, he received Eighteen Thousand Dollars
9 ($18,000.00) through Humphreys.

10       Drakulich testified that he did virtually nothing to
11 earn the commission and asked William Humphreys to handle the
12 matter for him because he, Drakulich, was busy and involved with
13 business in the legislature.

14
15                      III.
       THE CONFORTE SALE TO THE CONVENTION AUTHORITY

16
17     A)   The Conforte Proposal
18       After the purchase of the Capurro-Gault land by Joe
19 Conforte, Conforte began a public campaign to sell the center
20 portion of the land, located in the flood plain area, to a
21 public agency in Washoe County for the purpose of having a golf
22 course developed. Conforte told realtor James Smith that the
23 development of the golf course would enhance the value of the
24 adjoining property and he, Conforte, would reap a profit on the
25 future sale and development of the remaining property in an
26 amount in excess of One Million Dollars ($1,000,000.00). Other
27 witnesses confirmed the probability that Conforte would make
28 a huge profit.

-7-

Shortly after the purchase of the land by Mr. Conforte, Councilman James Vernon and Councilman Pete Lemberes actively sought to have the City of Sparks purchase the land from Conforte. However, the City of Sparks did not have sufficient financial resources to purchase the land and develop it into a golf course.

Subsequently, proposals were made to the Convention Authority offering to sell the land to them. Again, James Vernon, Chairman of the Convention Authority, was a strong advocate for the purchase of the Conforte land. In addition to Councilman James Vernon, Washoe County Commissioner Gerry Grow, a member and secretary of the Convention Authority, also strongly advocated the purchase of the Conforte land and the development of the golf course. Mr. Grow testified that he advocated the golf course because it would be a good addition to the golf courses already in existence in Washoe County and because he, an avid golfer himself, felt it was a good community investment for the Convention Authority.

The Convention Authority had, in the meantime, with the assistance of a citizens' advisory committee, set certain priorities for the expenditure of Convention Authority funds. The first priority set by the Board was the erection of an addition to the Centennial Coliseum which would be used, for among other things, the upcoming National Bowling Congress meeting. In order to obtain that convention, the Convention Authority had to give assurances that such a facility would be built because it was anticipated that there would be as many as 25,000 participants who would be present in the Reno area for

several weeks.  The second priority set by the Board was the
purchase of the land for the purpose of a golf course in Sparks.
The revenues of the Convention Authority were not sufficient to
finance both priorities.  As time passed, the golf course became
the first priority, replacing the addition to the Centennial
Coliseum.

### B)  The Room Tax Increase

Commissioner Gerry Grow advocated a one cent increase
in the room tax which is collected from lodgings in the Reno-
Sparks area.  In order for the room tax to be increased, it was
necessary that the increase be approved by all three governing
bodies in Washoe County; the Reno City Council, the Sparks City
Council, and the Washoe County Commission.  The increase was
first passed by the Washoe County Commission and the Sparks
City Council.

The Reno City Council first voted on the room tax
increase on the 25th day of March, 1974.  James Vernon and Gerry
Grow appeared at the Reno City Council meeting and urged passage
of the one cent increase in the room tax.  The vote resulted in
a tie.  During the vote, Reno Councilman Clyde Biglieri abstained.
The reason he gave for abstaining was that he had an interest
in a motel and thus felt it was a conflict of interest for him
to vote.

On May 13th and May 20th, 1974, the issue was brought
before the Reno City Council with little public notice.  Several
interested parties complained about the lack of notice on such
an important issue.

On August 12, 1974, the issue was again before the Council and the roll call vote again resulted in a tie. Councilman Biglieri, who abstained, said if he were to vote, he would favor the proposed increase. After the vote ended in a tie, he said that he was going to change his abstention and vote on the issue. Biglieri then voted in favor of the room tax increase. The increase was thereby approved.

Upon passage of the room tax increase, long term financing was available to make it possible for the Convention Authority to fund the addition to the Centennial Coliseum and to fund the Conforte golf course.

Mr. Biglieri explained that he felt that because Mayor Sam Dibitonto, a hotel owner, voted he, Biglieri, felt justified in voting rather than abstaining. Biglieri testified that he favored the room tax increase because he believed that more money was needed to promote Reno. He said he was aware of the fact that a substantial portion of the money was going to be used to purchase the property owned by Conforte, the same property from which he, James Smith, and Washoe Realty had received a Forty Thousand Dollar ($40,000.00) sales commission. He stated that the fact that he had received a commission from the Conforte land purchase did not influence his vote. He also testified that although he had several meetings with and phone calls from Joe Conforte urging him to vote in favor of the room tax increase, that those contacts also had no effect on his vote. When asked whether or not there was any arrangement to the effect that Biglieri and Washoe Realty would receive future real estate business from Conforte in the sale of the property

-10-

1  surrounding the golf course retained by Conforte, Biglieri

2  testified that there was no arrangement to that effect, but

3  that he would accept the opportunity to sell the land if it

4  were offered to him by Conforte.

5      Joe Choma, associated with Councilman Biglieri at

6  Washoe Realty, testified that he had a vague recollection that

7  they, Washoe Realty and Clyde Biglieri, might be involved in

8  the sale of Conforte's property in the future.

9

10  C)  **The Proposal to Change the Composition of the Convention Authority - Senate Bill 152**

11      The Grand Jury found that on February 28, 1973, former

12  Senator Stanley Drakulich appeared at the regular meeting of the

13  Washoe County Fair and Recreation Board (Convention Authority)

14  and spoke in opposition to Senate Bill 152, (Exhibit No. 10),

15  which would have increased the size of the Convention Authority

16  to include four members in addition to the five elected public

17  officials.  The Board voted to oppose SB 152 after a promise of

18  more cooperation with the Chamber of Commerce.  The Chamber,

19  sponsor of SB 152, agreed to withdraw the legislation.

20      Former Senator Stanley Drakulich testified that his

21  opposition to the expansion of the membership of the Convention

22  Authority was in no way related to his receiving the Eighteen

23  Thousand Dollar ($18,000.00) commission from Joe Conforte in

24  connection with Conforte's purchase of the Capurro-Gault land.

25  Drakulich testified that he had opposed the expansion of the

26  Convention Authority because he did not want the Chamber of

27  Commerce to have added representation.  He felt that the present

28  composition of the Convention Authority was adequate and superior

to the proposed expanded Convention Authority.

### D)  The Conforte Repurchase Agreement

The golf course portion of Conforte's land was purchased by the Convention Authority and Washoe County took title to the property upon the following conditions contained in the escrow documents.

> "If within five (5) years from the date of purchase, buyer, its successors, assigns, grantees or permittees shall not have in good faith commenced construction of an 18 hole public golf course on said lands, and, if buyer commences a sale of said land or a part thereof pursuant to NRS 244.281, sellers, their heirs or as- signees, shall have the right to meet or better the terms of any bid on said land submitted by any third party at any such sale."

(Exhibit No. 11)

Thus, Conforte was assured that either a golf course would be built at public expense or he could exercise his option to repurchase the land he sold to the Convention Authority.

### E)  Execution of the Sale Agreement

After the details of the purchase agreement were resolved, the agreement was approved by the Convention Authority and executed by James Vernon, Convention Authority Chairman, and Gerry Grow, Secretary of the Convention Authority.

At the time when the final paperwork was available for signature, Commissioner Gerry Grow was in the State of Washington on a vacation. At that time, Conforte chartered a private plane and flew to Spokane, Washington, to return Mr. Grow to Reno for the purpose of signing the papers. Mr. Grow testified that although he could have waited until he completed his vacation and returned to Reno, that he returned early with Mr. Conforte to save him interest payments on the property. After Grow signed the documents, Conforte bought him an airline ticket back to Spokane. Grow also accepted One Hundred Dollars ($100.00) from Conforte for the inconvenience occasioned to his vacation. The Grand Jury finds this conduct of Mr. Grow to be consistent with the close personal relationship existing between some public officials and Conforte at the time of the land sale.

## IV.
## UNDISCLOSED INVOLVEMENT OF CONFORTE IN LOCAL PUBLIC AFFAIRS

Joe Conforte's involvement with the public officials most directly concerned in the acquisition of his Sparks property has been shown in other portions of this report and, at the least, it is clear that he encouraged both the sale of his land to the Convention Authority and the passage of the room tax increase which would finance the land purchase. However, during the course of the Grand Jury's investigation, there was evidence that Conforte's interest in major decisions by local public officials extended well beyond the sale of his Sparks property.

The Grand Jury found that at the time when the City of Reno was considering the appointment of Reno's Police Chief, that Conforte supported and encouraged the appointment of Colonel Alex Lamberes as Chief. The Grand Jury's evidence showed nothing more than a friendship between Colonel Lemberes and Conforte and the Grand Jury finds no improper motive or purpose behind Mr. Conforte's support of Colonel Lemberes. Also, Lemberes was apparently not seriously considered for the position because, among other reasons, of his lack of experience in civilian law enforcement. However, what is significant to the Grand Jury is that Mr. Conforte's involvement in local politics extended to the point of making private recommendations concerning such an important appointive position as Reno Police Chief.

The Grand Jury also found that Conforte encouraged members of the Sparks City Council to support the proposed salary increase for Judge Morrison of the Sparks Municipal Court. Judge Morrison's salary was later substantially increased.

The Grand Jury received evidence that at the time when former Reno City Councilman Sam Dibitonto was seeking the position of Mayor of the City of Reno he was contacted by Conforte. The Mayor is chosen by vote of the members of the Reno City Council. Mr. Dibitonto testified that when he was approached by Conforte, he was told that if he would make certain committee appointments, he could count on becoming Mayor. Dibitonto made no agreements with Conforte, but indicated that he would consider all of the council members for the committee appointments. After Dibitonto became Mayor, he made the particular committee appointments of concern to Conforte. However, he did not appoint those council members requested by Conforte. Thereafter, Conforte contacted Dibitonto, accused Dibitonto of turning him around, and expressed unhappiness with the appointments Dibitonto made.

-14-

appendix a

1   The Grand Jury also received other evidence that
2   Conforte was unhappy with Dibitonto and wanted him out of office.
3   The Grand Jury wishes to stress, however, that it received no
4   evidence that Mr. Dibitonto's successor in office, who defeated
5   him in the last election, was a candidate who was being supported
6   by Conforte and certainly no inferences should be drawn against
7   Mr. Dibitonto's successor.

8       The Grand Jury makes note that in these two instances
9   where Conforte supported certain appointments for important
10  official positions, those appointments were not made.  Nonethe-
11  less, it is apparent to the Grand Jury and the Grand Jury finds
12  that Mr. Conforte's relationship with certain local officials
13  reached a point where he believed that he had some considerable
14  effect upon decisions relative to official action.  The Grand
15  Jury cites these examples not as any kind of criticism of the
16  people being supported, but rather as a reflection of the formerly
17  undisclosed scope of Conforte's attempted involvement in the
18  public's business.

19
20              V.
        CONFORTE'S ASSOCIATION WITH PUBLIC
        OFFICIALS INVOLVED WITH THE LAND SALE
21
22      A)  The Mustang Meetings
23      The Washoe County Grand Jury has investigated the
24  relationship of Joe Conforte with the various public officials
25  connected with the land transaction and finds the following:
26      During the time that the Conforte land transaction was
27  pending before the three local governing bodies and the Convention
28  Authority, James Vernon, Gerry Grow and Pete Lemberes regularly

-15-

117

visited Joe Conforte's Mustang brothel. At that time, Vernon
was the Convention Authority Chairman and a Sparks Councilman,
Grow was the Convention Authority secretary and a Washoe County
Commissioner, and Lemberes was a Sparks Councilman. At several
of these Mustang visits, the three met with Conforte and public
business was discussed.

The Grand Jury has received testimony from Vernon,
Lemberes and Grow that they would enter the Mustang complex and
instead of going to the public reception area, they would go to
a special area of the brothel where food, drink, and the services
of prostitutes were available to them free of charge. On occasion, other public officials and guests went to the brothel
with Vernon, Lemberes and Grow.

In addition to the testimony of Vernon, Grow and
Lemberes, the above finding was verified by other witnesses
before the Grand Jury. Vernon, Grow and Lemberes were on
Conforte's "comp list" at the brothel. Additionally, meetings
were held by the three with Conforte on occasion at locations
other than the brothel.

At one meeting at the brothel attended by Conforte,
Vernon, Lemberes and Grow on Conforte's birthday, Conforte
discussed getting the "right people" in public office. They
also discussed the one cent room tax increase and it was
suggested that they "get rid" of Mayor Dibitonto because he was
the one who was stopping the room tax from going through.

The Grand Jury's investigation has also revealed that
Mustang prostitutes attended a party for local public officials
held by Pete Lemberes at his Sparks residence.

-16-

Commissioner Grow testified that the Mustang meetings had no effect upon his judgment regarding matters pending before the Convention Authority and the Washoe County Commission. He also defended the receipt of complimentary services of prostitutes as being no different than receiving a complimentary meal from a local casino. A Grand Juror asked Mr. Grow whether he thought the public would accept his, Grow's, rationalization of their conduct at Mustang. Mr. Grow responded, "I don't care if they do or not," and added that he might not run for re-election next term anyway.

B)  Conforte Campaign Contributions

In addition to the contacts of Joe Conforte with the above mentioned public figures, the Washoe County Grand Jury has determined that Joe Conforte spends large amounts of money each election in the form of campaign contributions and other assistance to political candidates. Also, Joe Conforte has paid at least $3,000.00 to $4,000.00 each election year for the results of a local political poll conducted by Mr. Brent Tyler.

The Grand Jury has inquired into campaign contributions made by Joe Conforte to key public officials who served on the Convention Authority, supported the Conforte land transaction, or were otherwise found in the course of the Jury's investigation to be associated with Joe Conforte. Although the Grand Jury has not at this time conducted any major inquiry into campaign contributions received by public officials in Washoe County, a future Grand Jury may wish to probe further into Mr. Conforte's involvement in and influence in public af-

- 17 -

119

fairs in Washoe County.

Mr. Clyde Biglieri, Reno City Councilman, testified that he was contacted by Pete Lemberes and James Vernon and was taken to Mustang where he received a Five Hundred Dollar ($500.00) campaign contribution from Joe Conforte.

Mr. Roy Pagni, former Washoe County Commissioner, also a member of the Convention Authority at the time of the purchase of the Conforte land, testified that he received Two Thousand Dollars ($2,000.00) during his last political campaign.

Mr. Michael Schultz, former Sparks Councilman, testified that when he first ran for the Sparks City Council, he was contacted by Councilman James Vernon who offered Conforte aid in Schultz's campaign. At first Schultz declined, but later he asked for and received Two Hundred Dollars ($200.00) from Conforte.

Mr. Carl Bogart, Reno Mayor and Convention Authority member, received One Thousand One Hundred Fifty Five Dollars and ninety-eight cents ($1,155.98) during his last campaign from Joe Conforte.

At his first appearance before the Washoe County Grand Jury, Mayor Carl Bogart was asked if Conforte ever contributed to his campaign. He said, "Yes." When asked how much was contributed he said he couldn't answer that because the contributions came directly to his campaign manager and although that campaign manager gave him a list of his contributions, he couldn't remember the specific figures. He testified that he had no idea how much Conforte had given him.

Later, Mayor Bogart claimed that he did not receive any of Conforte's money. He explained that in his prior testimony he was merely referring to the fact that Conforte had said that he would help Bogart in his campaign. Bogart said he told Conforte to keep everything above board. According to Bogart, he told Conforte that he had hired a campaign manager. Bogart then said he heard nothing more about any Conforte contributions.

Mayor Bogart was contradicted by his campaign manager. He testified that he did not receive the bulk of the contributions in Mr. Bogart's campaign, but rather that Bogart himself received most of the contributions. Among those contributions received by Bogart's campaign manager were two contributions, one in the amount of Eight Hundred Sixty Six Dollars and seventy-eight cents ($866.78) and another in the amount of Two Hundred Eighty Nine Dollars and twenty cents ($289.20) for a total of One Thousand One Hundred Fifty Five Dollars and ninety-eight cents ($1,155.98). These checks were received from political pollster Brent Tyler. The campaign manager indicated that he was not sure of the original source of the two checks from Brent Tyler, but assumed that they were from Joe Conforte.

Political pollster Brent Tyler testified that those two contributions, in a total amount of One Thousand One Hundred Fifty Five Dollars and ninety-eight cents ($1,155.98), were made to Bogart by Conforte. Tyler testified that he and Bogart had discussed the contributions and that he, Tyler, solicited the money from Conforte with Bogart's permission and approval. At the time, according to Tyler, Bogart said that he did not care that people knew about the solicitations from Conforte.

WITH MALICE TOWARD ONE

1　　　There is also evidence that Conforte has given other
2　gratuities to public officials.
3　　　Although not a campaign contribution, in August of
4　1972 former Councilman Pete Lemberes bought Joe Conforte's 1972
5　Lincoln Continental Mark IV. Mr. Lemberes testified that he
6　paid Seven Thousand Five Hundred Dollars ($7,500.00) cash for the
7　Conforte car and received no bill of sale, papers or receipt
8　other than a Department of Motor Vehicles green slip.
9　and its actions.

-20-

~~Accordingly, lines 10 through 28, page 20 and~~
~~through 20, page 21, of the report are hereby stricken.~~

21　　　The Grand Jury is charged with the responsibility of
22　inquiring into allegations of official misconduct. In follow-
23　ing this mandate, the Grand Jury has used every available means
24　to obtain the truth in its inquiry, an inquiry which has con-
25　tinued for nearly two years. After answering the Grand Jury's
26　questions, every witness has been given the opportunity to have
27　his say and has been given the opportunity to present whatever
28　evidence he wishes.

-21-

122

Furthermore, the Grand Jury is confident that the community will find that the efforts expended in making this inquiry were worthwhile, productive, and in the best interests of the citizens of Washoe County.

## VI.
## THE CONFORTE LAND TRANSACTION
## AND THE PUBLIC'S INTEREST

### A) Conflict of Interest and the Need for Disclosure

The Convention Authority's purchase of Conforte's property is illustrative of the problems of conflict of interest which arise when officials fail to disclose their interest in matters pending before public agencies. The Grand Jury finds that such failure to disclose possible conflicts of interest cloud the reputation and integrity of the public official himself. Such non-disclosure also has the natural effect of increasing the cynicism of the citizenry, many of whom are already disillusioned with the performance of governmental officials.

The Grand Jury recommends that a public official regard his office as a public trust and always do everything in his power to avoid the appearance of impropriety. Public office should not be used to assist friends or amass wealth. To instill public confidence in government, officials should at all times act openly and in the best interest of the public. When a conflict of interest does exist, the public official should always reveal not only the conflict but all of the reasons for the conflict.

-22-

B) <u>Former Sparks Councilman Vernon, former
Sparks Councilman Lemberes, and Commissioner
Grow</u>

The Grand Jury finds, in consideration of all of its
other findings in this investigation, that the manner in which
the Conforte land transaction was conducted was not in the
public's best interest.

The Grand Jury further finds that former Sparks
Councilmen James Vernon and Pete Lemberes and Washoe County
Commissioner Gerry Grow were closely involved with Joe Conforte.
At the same time, they did not disclose to the public their
relationship with Conforte and proceeded to actively crusade
to have public agencies purchase Conforte's property knowing
that Conforte would realize huge profits if the sale were
consummated. In so acting these public officials failed to
honor a trust which had been placed in them by the citizens
and voters of their respective constituencies.

As mentioned in the preface of this report, in
reaching these findings, this is not to suggest that Vernon,
Lemberes and Grow are guilty of criminal activity. However,
it is clear to the Grand Jury and the Grand Jury finds that
these public officials have by their actions not served the
public's best interest.

The Grand Jury also finds the purchase of the
Conforte land and the agreement to develop a golf course were
not handled in a businesslike fashion. The Grand Jury does
not substitute its own judgment on the merits of the purchase;
however, the Jury is alarmed at the apparent slipshod handling
by the Convention Authority of this important matter. Not only

1 did the Convention Authority accept a vague and indefinite
2 proposal without careful study, but the Authority members worked
3 headlong into an increase in the room tax and urged their fellow
4 elected public officials into passing the increase when no one
5 knew for sure how much money was needed or would be used for
6 pending Convention Authority projects. It appears that many
7 people were encouraged to submit requests for Convention Authori-
8 ty funds in order to engender public support for and justify the
9 tax increase when there was no definite plan or commitment to
10 fund any projects other than the purchase of the Conforte land
11 and the Coliseum expansion. Even as late as February 1976, it
12 had not yet been decided which public agency will bear the
13 expense of operating and maintaining the golf course.

14 Former Mayor Sam Dibitonto expressed some of the
15 findings of the Grand Jury when he said the following at a
16 Convention Authority meeting on April 26, 1974:

17 "We're sitting here ready to spend a
million point some dollars and you don't even
18 know what you're buying. Why you haven't got
any idea what the contract stipulations are.
19 You don't know what the time frame is. You
don't know anything. We're just bound and
20 determined we're going to buy 209 acres so
that we can make the other four and a half
21 or five, or whatever percentage, worth a ton
of money. Now, I think before we sit down
22 and spend this kind of money; now, you may
in your own mind be firmly convinced, but I
23 am responsible to people that are going to
have to pay this, and I don't like to spend
24 twenty bucks, let alone a million point two,
unless I get Mr. Torvinen to tell me what the
25 hell we're buying. Now, if you want to go vote
for it; you guys have got me snowed and you've
26 got me outnumbered, so I just thought I'd tell
you for the record that this is a tremendous
27 way to do business. I've never been on a
Board in my life that's done it this way."

28

-24-

125

Notwithstanding Mayor Dibitonto's statement, the other Convention Authority members proceeded to approve the acquisition. Those members were County Commissioners Grow and Pagni, Sparks Councilman Vernon, and Reno Councilman Carl Bogart. Although not a member of the Convention Authority, Sparks Councilman Lemberes was also present and expressed his strong support for the acquisition. Not only has the Convention Authority spent approximately Nine Hundred Eighty Thousand Dollars ($980,000.00) for the golf course property, but an additional One Million Five Hundred Thousand Dollars ($1,500,000.00) to Two Million Dollars ($2,000,000.00) will be needed to develop the golf course, erect necessary buildings and purchase equipment.

As a result of the Convention Authority's acquisition of the Conforte property, and assuming that a golf course is developed as planned, according to testimony before the Grand Jury, Conforte may make over One Million Dollars ($1,000,000.00) in profit.

C) **Former State Senator Stanley Drakulich**

In the case of former State Senator Stanley Drakulich, the Grand Jury finds that he, by his actions in concealing his involvement in the Conforte-Capurro land transaction, did not act in the public's best interest. There is no good reason for his failure to be listed in the official documents of the land transaction as being one who received monies. Furthermore, Mr. Drakulich failed to be forthright and open concerning the Eighteen Thousand Dollar ($18,000.00) payment to him from Mr. Conforte. Only after the payment was disclosed by the media did

-25-

1  he, Drakulich, acknowledge receiving it.

2      It is not in the public's best interest when any public

3  official receives an extraordinarily large fee for doing very

4  little and further attempts to conceal such a fact from the

5  public when the public itself is involved.

6

7      D)  **Councilman Clyde Biglieri**

8      Councilman Biglieri's real estate firm handled the

Conforte land transaction and Councilman Biglieri received a

9  large commission from Conforte as a result of the transaction.

10  Thereafter, when he broke the tie vote and cast the decisive

11  vote on the room tax increase, Mr. Biglieri was aware that a

12  substantial portion of the revenue from the tax increase would

13  be used by the Convention Authority to purchase the same land

14  from Conforte and that Conforte was in a position to make major

15  profits from the transaction.

16      The Grand Jury finds that a conflict of interest

17  existed when Councilman Biglieri voted for the room tax increase.

18  The conflict of interest arose from the Forty Thousand Dollar

19  ($40,000.00) commission that Mr. Biglieri and his associate

20  received from Conforte when Conforte purchased the Capurro

21  property approximately one year earlier.[*] Also, Councilman

22  Biglieri's action in voting on the room tax increase was obvious-

23  ly inconsistent with his twice earlier voluntary disqualification

24  of himself on the same vote.

25  _____

26      [*] It should be noted that these actions occurred before
the criminal conflict of interest law was enacted in the 1975
27  legislative session and went into effect in July of 1975.

28

1   Further considerations relevant to Mr. Biglieri's
2   conflict of interest are that he received a substantial campaign
3   contribution from Joe Conforte, was urged to vote favorably
4   upon the issue by Conforte, and knew he had a chance of
5   receiving extensive Conforte business in connection with the
6   future sale and development of the parcel of land retained by
7   Conforte.

8   The Grand Jury recommends that public officials
9   assume an affirmative duty to be public watchdogs and alert the
10  public at large when other public officials are involved in
11  unusual transactions. Although he knew of the Drakulich
12  involvement at all times, Councilman Biglieri failed to alert
13  the public to the fact that Drakulich, a State Senator, had
14  received an Eighteen Thousand Dollar ($18,000.00) commission
15  from Joe Conforte when he, Drakulich, had done nothing to earn
16  it.

17

18  EXPANDING CONFORTE RELATIONSHIP WITH PUBLIC OFFICIALS

19

20  Of major concern to the Grand Jury is the expanding
21  and rather secretive relationships which have developed between
22  Joe Conforte and some public officials in this area.  In 1962,
23  Mr. Conforte was convicted of the felony offense of Extortion
24  of the then Washoe County District Attorney, William Raggio, and
25  was sentenced to three to five years in the Nevada State Prison.
26  In 1963, Conforte was also convicted of the federal felony of-
27  fense of Income Tax Evasion by Means of a Fraudulent Tax Return
28  and was sentenced to federal prison for a term of three years.

- 27 -

128

appendix a

Since release from prison, Conforte's primary source
of income has obviously been prostitution and he operates what
is probably the largest public house of prostitution in the
United States.  The Grand Jury has also discovered that many of
Conforte's close associates are ex-felons who have been convicted
of serious offenses in the State of Nevada and elsewhere.

The Grand Jury's investigation of the Conforte land
sale reveals that Mr. Conforte established substantial contacts
and rapport with a number of the public officials who were
directly involved in the land sale.  It is apparent that he
either contributed heavily to their political campaigns or
granted them other favors or gratuities as in the case of four
of the five members of the Convention Authority.  Not only did
Conforte have this relationship with a majority of the members
of the Convention Authority, but that those members also
represented the Sparks City Council, Reno City Council, and the
Washoe County Commission.  These are the three governmental
entities which make virtually all decisions bearing upon the
public's welfare in Washoe County.

Additionally, other evidence discloses that at the
time of the Conforte land sale, Mr. Conforte also held similar
associations with Sparks City Councilman Lemberes and Reno City
Councilman Biglieri.  It appears that through this spreading
association with local public officials, Conforte has gone so
far as to attempt to influence some of these public officials
to act in his favor and, in at least one instance, attempted to
influence them to consider a police chief for the City of Reno
of his choosing.

129

The Grand Jury's investigation has essentially focused
upon the Conforte land sale and Sparks government. With the
exception of former State Senator Stanley Drakulich, the Grand
Jury has not investigated or inquired into the role of Mr.
Conforte in regard to other local officials such as senators,
assemblymen, other city and county officers and statewide
officers. However, from evidence adduced before the Grand Jury,
it appears that at the least, Mr. Conforte has been an active
supporter of either some of these office holders or of political
candidates who unsuccessfully vied for such offices in recent
elections. The Jury recognizes that such support is an absolute
right and certainly within the prerogative of Mr. Conforte.
However, based on the experience of this investigation, it
appears that the local officials who have been involved with
Conforte have done so without disclosing this relationship to
the public.               -29-
                                    3

The judgment of this Court entered on the 21st day of
April 1977, having been reversed in part by the Supreme Court
of the State of Nevada on February 16, 1979, and it appearing
that no formal modification has been entered in accordance with
the order of the Supreme Court, IT IS HEREBY ORDERED that
lines 17 through 28, page 29, and lines 1 through 6, page 30, of
the Report of the Washoe County Grand Jury, dated March 15, 1976,
be and the same hereby are expunged.

Dated this 16th day of March, 1981.

                              *William H. Forman*
                              District Judge

Considering the Jury's findings in this investigation,
the Grand Jurors find such spreading and undisclosed relationships definitely not to be in the best interests of good government or an educated public. It is the recommendation of this
Grand Jury that all public officials who have received financial
support or other favors from Mr. Conforte or other persons
having a financial interest in pending public matters should
voluntarily disclose these relationships to the public. It is
also recommended that such relationships, especially where they
have not been publicly disclosed, be considered for review in
future years.

THE MUSTANG BROTHEL AND ITS EFFECT ON WASHOE COUNTY

I.
THE HEALTH HAZARD

Joe Conforte's presence in public affairs in Washoe
County is very evident from the foregoing descriptions of his
activities. The presence of prostitutes in Storey County is
also apparent in Washoe County.

The Grand Jury has received evidence from a State
Health official that there is virtually no State inspection or
regulation of Nevada brothels. Only when a case of venereal
disease is reported to State authorities by a local doctor does

1 the State Health Department become involved in tracing the

2 disease and requiring treatment of it. Because of the nature

3 of the prostitution business, few, if any, patrons of a diseased

4 prostitute can be traced. The patron and his intimate contacts,

5 as a practical matter, cannot be contacted by the Health

6 Department and informed that they have been exposed to venereal

7 disease.

8 Although a private physician is hired by the

9 prostitutes and Joe Conforte, in some instances the disease is

10 not discovered for up to thirty days after it is contracted by

11 the prostitutes. If the prostitute has only ten contacts a day,

12 five days a week, 200 patrons could be infected.

13 Mr. Robert DelCarlo, Sheriff of Storey County,

14 testified before the Grand Jury that although between thirty and

15 fifty prostitutes work at the Mustang brothel, no Storey County

16 officials enforce health laws in Storey County or in any way

17 inspect the Mustang brothel. The only enforcement that takes

18 place is the registration of prostitutes by Sheriff DelCarlo's

19 officers. However, he testified that the Sheriff's Department

20 only registers prostitutes every thirty to sixty days. Thus,

21 a prostitute could work for thirty to sixty days before being

22 registered. Sheriff DelCarlo admitted that during a one year

23 period in 1974 and 1975, he and his office did not register any

24 prostitutes or check the prostitutes to see if they had work

25 permits.

26 Also, Sheriff DelCarlo admitted that the registration

27 process as practiced in Storey County is of little value. He

28 testified that he allows the prostitutes to give names other

than their true names. He also admitted that no real effort is made to correctly identify the prostitutes or check their respective backgrounds. Further, he testified that no applicant has ever been denied permission to work at the Mustang brothel for any reason.

## II.
## SOLICITATION AND PANDERING

During the course of the Grand Jury's investigation, a qualified witness estimated that 75 percent of the Mustang brothel's business comes from the Reno area. Many of those customers are tourists who are driven to Mustang in taxi cabs. Taxi drivers receive 30 percent of whatever is spent by the customer at the brothel.

As a result of the financial inducements offered to cab drivers, bell hops, etc., there is a danger of widespread solicitation and pandering taking place within Washoe County where prostitution is illegal.

There is also evidence of prostitutes traveling to Washoe County from Storey County and on occasion performing their services in residences, hotels and motels.

The members of the Grand Jury find that State, County and City statutes and ordinances are not adequate to control prostitution, solicitation and pandering that takes place in Washoe County. Thus, the Grand Jury recommends that the respective governmental agencies act to provide effective laws to control prostitution, pandering and solicitation in Washoe County.

- 12 -

The Washoe County Grand Jury finds that prostitution
in Storey County constitutes a health and safety hazard to
Washoe County because of Storey County's failure to adequately
supervise, inspect and identify the prostitutes. Since the
prostitutes are allowed to give false names and are not required
to identify themselves adequately for the purposes of health
inspections and other legitimate inquiries, the residents of
adjoining counties are not adequately protected from the
potential health hazards posed by the Mustang prostitutes.

### III.
### CONFORTE'S UNDERWORLD CONTACTS AND THEIR EFFECT ON WASHOE COUNTY

The Grand Jury finds that Mustang employees and their
associates have a tendency to be involved in crimes including
property crimes and drug traffic in Washoe County. It is
important for Washoe County and other counties and state law
enforcement agencies to keep track of these people and to know
their true identities and whereabouts.

The Grand Jury finds that Joe Conforte has associated
with known and suspected organized crime figures from various
parts of the United States. Furthermore, he has employed,
consorted with, and been a friend of many ex-felons. Among those
he has associated with and employed are ex-felons who have been
convicted in Washoe County and elsewhere of crimes ranging from
armed robbery to burglary, grand larceny, drug offenses and
other serious offenses.

Although Mr. Conforte, himself an ex-felon, is free to
associate with whomever he wishes, and although the above as-

-33-

sociations do not constitute a violation of criminal law by
Conforte, it is apparent from the evidence received by the
Grand Jury and the Grand Jury finds that Conforte and his
prostitution business attract an undesirable element which poses
a threat to the safety and welfare of the citizens of Washoe
County.

This Grand Jury has chosen not to pass upon the wisdom
of allowing prostitution in the State of Nevada. However, in
light of its findings in this report, the Grand Jury recommends
that if prostitution is to be continued within Nevada, that
State Legislators representing Washoe County consider supporting
laws which would create restrictions and controls upon the
prostitution industry which would protect the health, safety
and welfare of the citizens of the State.

### SPARKS MUNICIPAL COURT, JUDGE MORRISON

The Washoe County Grand Jury has received testimony
that former Sparks Councilmen James Vernon, Pete Lemberes and
Michael Schultz have on occasion approached Judge Morrison
and received dismissals or reductions of traffic charges pending
before the Court against other persons.

Judge Morrison testified that former Councilman
Lemberes spoke to him about seven or eight pending cases and at
Lemberes' request, Morrison dismissed the cases.

Morrison testified that he was likewise approached by
former Councilman James Vernon regarding matters pending before
the Court twelve to fifteen times and he, Morrison, dismissed

- 14 -

1   eight or nine of those cases.

2      Also, according to Judge Morrison, on two occasions
3 former Sparks Councilman Michael Schultz requested the reduction
4 of cases involving a friend. Charges were reduced in both cases.

5      After having been approached by those Councilmen,
6 Judge Morrison asked some of the defendants to come in and speak
7 to him on the issues. On several occasions, he dismissed cases
8 without asking the defendants to come in at all.

9      There is also evidence which suggests that there have
10 been reductions and dismissals granted at the request of the
11 Sparks Police Department.

12      The Washoe County Grand Jury could find no payment or
13 other consideration given for the dismissals and, therefore,
14 finds that no crime has been committed. The Grand Jury firmly
15 believes that the judiciary on all levels should not in any
16 way allow other public officials to influence its decisions on
17 pending court matters. It is this sort of partiality which
18 gives rise to much of the criticism levied against the criminal
19 justice system.

20

21   GENERAL ACCEPTANCE CORPORATION - HOSPITALITY HUT

22

23      During the month of April 1972, former State Senator
24 Stanley Drakulich came to the office of Jerry Higgins, Com-
25 munity Relations Director for the Sparks Nugget. Drakulich told
26 Higgins that he, Drakulich, knew the relationship between the
27 Nugget and Councilman Vernon and Councilman Lemberes was not
28 good. Drakulich said he felt he could help the Nugget improve

-35-

their relationship with Vernon and Lemberes. In the conversation, Drakulich mentioned that he was employed by General Acceptance Corporation (G.A.C.) and would like to establish a land sales booth in the Nugget casino. Drakulich was told that the Nugget's floor space was at a premium and that officials of the casino would not favor such an idea, but Mr. Higgins assured Drakulich that he would set up a meeting with John Ascuaga so Drakulich could discuss the land sales booth with Mr. Ascuaga.

Shortly thereafter, Mr. Higgins received a phone call from Drakulich. He asked Jerry Higgins to have lunch with Sparks Councilman Vernon and Councilman Lemberes the next day at the Sambos Restaurant in Sparks. At the meeting, Vernon, Lemberes and Drakulich said they would like to improve their relationship with the Nugget. Higgins told them that he hoped the Nugget did have a good relationship with them. Higgins was again asked if he would set up the meeting with John Ascuaga and Pete Carr so Stan Drakulich could discuss putting a land sales booth in the Nugget.

Jerry Higgins discussed Drakulich's proposal with John Ascuaga. Mr. Ascuaga was opposed to the land sales promotion being associated with the Nugget; however, he agreed to meet with Drakulich.

Later, Mr. Higgins received a call at home from James Vernon who said he was attending a party at the Rodeway Inn. Vernon asked Higgins to pave the way for the Drakulich meeting with John Ascuaga the next day. Vernon said that if Higgins would help the Senator get his land sales booth, the Nugget's troubles with the Sparks City Council would be over. Higgins told Vernon that he would set up the meeting, but that he couldn't assure Vernon of anything regarding the land sales booth.

Approximately five minutes later, Higgins received a call from Pete Lemberes. Lemberes said he was as the same party at the Rodeway Inn. He also asked Higgins to do what he could to help the Senator. Lemberes also said he thought the Nugget should run some insurance business Stan's way and "let him make a buck." The meeting was set up the next day and Stan Drakulich and a representative from G.A.C. met with John Ascuaga. Mr. Ascuaga told Drakulich and the representative from G.A.C. that he would not allow the land sales business in the Sparks Nugget.

Drakulich was perturbed when Ascuaga turned him down. Drakulich later told a member of the Nugget's management, "I will get Mr. Ascuaga one way or another."

About a week later, a member of the Nugget management received information that there was going to be a G.A.C. Hospitality Booth placed on City property in front of the Nugget and that the proposal was scheduled before the Sparks City Council. Nugget officials immediately contacted their attorney. He represented them at the Sparks City Council meeting held on June 12, 1972, and opposed the proposed placement of the Hospitality Hut on City property arguing that such an arrangement would be an illegal use of City property. Sparks City Attorney Paul Freitag agreed that it would be illegal for

- 37 -

137

the City to use the property in the proposed manner. Councilman
Vernon and Councilman Lemberes supported the proposal, but it
was nevertheless defeated.

After the meeting, the Nugget's attorney and Nugget
officials left the building and were encountered by Stan
Drakulich in the parking lot. Drakulich said that they had the
last laugh this time, but the future would unveil secrets of
things to come or words to that effect. Drakulich was very
angry and upon being asked by the Nugget's attorney if he was
going to use his position of public trust as a State Senator
to try to get even with John Ascuaga, Drakulich said no, but
said he, Drakulich, was a "very hot bohunk."

The Grand Jury finds that this type of conduct by
public officials is clearly not in the public's best interest.

## LEMBERES' ATTEMPT TO REDUCE SALARY OF SPARKS CITY ATTORNEY PAUL FREITAG

The Washoe County Grand Jury subpoenaed former Councilman Pete Lemberes on several occasions during February of 1975.
He was questioned about several matters including some dealings
with Sparks City Attorney Paul Freitag.

On the 24th day of March, 1975, Pete Lemberes in a
speech before the Sparks City Council, viciously attacked Paul
Freitag suggesting that Mr. Freitag had engaged in improper
conduct. Lemberes then requested that Freitag draft an ordinance
that would reduce his, Freitag's, salary from $17,500.00 a
year to $10,000.00 per year.

-38-

At the first recess of the Council meeting on that date, Lemberes approached Freitag and said,

> "I hate to stab you in the back, but I don't like what I'm hearing from the Grand Jury. You have been singing like a bird."

The Washoe County Grand Jury has found no improper conduct by Sparks City Attorney Paul Freitag. He appeared and testified before the Grand Jury pursuant to subpoena and appeared to the Jurors to be both a truthful and candid witness.

The measure introduced by Lemberes was allowed to die without further action by Lemberes and other members of the Sparks City Council.

The Washoe County Grand Jury finds the conduct of Mr. Lemberes in this regard the same as a witness who appeared before the Sparks Council and spoke on Mr. Freitag's behalf during the hearing on the ordinance regarding Mr. Freitag's salary. The witness stated that the proposed amendment of Mr. Freitag's salary was ". . . a vicious exercise of raw political power."

### THE HELMS GRAVEL PIT

In 1968, Mr. Robert Helms, contractor and businessman, completed his purchase of a parcel of land bordering on the City of Sparks east of McCarran Boulevard and north of Interstate Highway 80. As a result of the sale of the property to Helms, the City of Sparks became a third party beneficiary to the sale. The agreement provided that Sparks was entitled to some portion

-19-

1  of the property when Helms completed his excavation of aggregate.

2  However, the terms of the agreement were not clearly defined and

3  the City of Sparks was not sufficiently informed as to what

4  portion of the land it was entitled to and when the land would

5  be conveyed to the City.  Therefore, it became necessary for

6  the City of Sparks to enter into negotiations to reach an agree-

7  ment concerning the rights and obligations of Helms and the

8  City of Sparks over the gravel pit property.

9        As a result of the Grand Jury's inquiry, the Grand Jury

10  became concerned that the City of Sparks had gone for such a

11  long period of time without any definition of its legal rights

12  and obligations regarding the gravel pit.  No agreement had been

13  negotiated with Mr. Helms and no law suit had been filed to

14  determine the parties' respective rights.  Only after the Grand

15  Jury began its inquiry in February of 1975 were intensive

16  negotiations begun.  An agreement between Helms and the City of

17  Sparks was executed January 12, 1976.

18        The Grand Jury finds that the Sparks City Council

19  and Sparks City Attorney were negligent in not insisting that

20  this important agreement with Mr. Helms be concluded more

21  rapidly.  A delay of more than six years is not diligent atten-

22  tion to a matter of such importance to the City of Sparks and

23  its citizens.

24        During the Grand Jury's inquiry into the status of

25  the gravel pit, located in what is rapidly becoming a residential

26  area of the City of Sparks, the Grand Jury found that Washoe

27  County was the local governmental entity which was responsible

28  for zoning and regulation of the Helms gravel pit.  This is

-40-

140

1 because the pit is still located within Washoe County and has
2 not been annexed into the City of Sparks. The Grand Jury was
3 surprised to find that the City of Sparks and Washoe County did
4 very little to study the effect of the pit upon the surrounding
5 property. There was varying testimony among experts who
6 testified before the Grand Jury concerning the effect of the
7 excavation on the water table in the adjacent area upon which
8 housing developments are located. There was also varying
9 testimony regarding the proper, safe, and acceptable slope of
10 the interior of the gravel pit.

11         It is apparent to the members of the Grand Jury that
12 little thought, study and investigation was given to the impact
13 of the gravel pit upon surrounding areas, both as to long term
14 effects and short term effects. This is particularly significant
15 in view of the Grand Jury's finding that the pit area is one of
16 the worst and most conspicuous eyesores in the entire Truckee
17 Meadows.

18         On the 18th day of March, 1968, Mr. Helms was granted
19 a special use permit by the Board of Adjustment of Washoe County.
20 The permit was granted on the condition that the excavation be
21 done in compliance with all applicable ordinances of Washoe
22 County, a $5,000.00 bond be posted and that the project be
23 reviewed in one year.

24         Mr. Helms has conducted his excavation of that property
25 since 1968. According to Mr. Robert Vice, Washoe County
26 Engineer, County records reveal only one formal inspection of the
27 pit, a year later in 1969.

28

-41-

141

The Grand Jury is critical of the fact that Washoe County, the Board of Adjustment and the Regional Planning Commission have failed to check, supervise and control property owners whose property is being used pursuant to special use permits. After those permits are issued, there does not appear to be any person or governmental agency in Washoe County which acts as an inspection and enforcement arm to assure the citizens of this community that the people operating under special use permits are in compliance with terms and conditions of their permits.

The Grand Jury finds that such a procedure can lead to alarming results in a rapidly growing community. The Grand Jury recommends that the Regional Planning Commission and the various governmental agencies in the County and City adopt procedures whereby special use permits and other variances and procedures allowed by the agencies on a temporary basis are reviewed and scrutinized from a planning standpoint periodically in order to insure the public that its interests are being served.

## THE DAIRY INDUSTRY IN WASHOE COUNTY

### I.
### REBATES AND ILLEGAL CONDUCT

During the course of the Grand Jury's investigation into the reported solicitation by former Sparks Councilman Vernon of Sid Doan for the milk account at Sierra Sid's Union 76 Station, the Washoe County Grand Jury subpoenaed Ronald

- 4 -

1   Averett from the Meadow Gold Milk Company. He appeared and
2   testified on the 22nd day of January, 1975. Among other things,
3   Averett testified that some wholesale milk dealers in the Reno
4   area and throughout Nevada were engaged in illegal conduct
5   including the giving of illegal rebates to retailers. This
6   information was later made public during a preliminary hearing
7   involving criminal charges against former Councilmen Vernon and
8   Lemberes, and has since been used by Attorney General Robert
9   List in challenging milk pricing and other dairy commission
10  practices in Nevada.

11          The Washoe County Grand Jury is pleased that it was
12  able to uncover these improper practices and believes that as
13  a result of the disclosure, hundreds of thousands of dollars
14  have been saved by Nevada consumers. This saving of consumers'
15  dollars alone appears to have far exceeded the total cost to
16  Washoe County taxpayers of the Grand Jury's entire investigation.

17          This discovery has also already led to valuable
18  reforms in Nevada's milk industry. In this regard, the Grand
19  Jury applauds the work of Attorney General List. His three-
20  part report on the dairy industry and the dairy commission is
21  an outstanding public service document which, hopefully, will
22  result in drastic changes and improvements in the regulation of
23  the dairy industry in Nevada.

24

25                              II.
            OFFER OF A MILK SALES CONTRACT TO SID DOAN'S
26           SIERRA 76 TRUCK STOP BY COUNCILMAN VERNON

27          As a major part of its investigation into Sparks
28  government, the Grand Jury investigated an alleged incident

                              - 4 3 -

involving the offer of a milk sales contract by Sparks Councilman and Meadow Gold salesman James Vernon to Sid Doan of Sierra Sid's 76 Truck Stop in Sparks. The evidence regarding this portion of the Grand Jury's investigation and regarding other dairy product transactions was directed to the attention of the Washoe County District Attorney for consideration of whether prosecution should be undertaken by the District Attorney prior to completion of the Grand Jury's investigation. Subsequently, the District Attorney authorized the filing of a criminal complaint against former Councilmen James Vernon and Pete Lemberes. Because that prosecution is still pending, the Grand Jury, on the advice of the Washoe County District Attorney's Office, will make no comment at this time concerning its investigation into these matters.

## SUTTER HILL SHOPPING CENTER

The Washoe County Grand Jury has spent considerable time investigating the land sale transaction in which the property located at the corner of McCarran Boulevard and Prater Way was ultimately sold to the Sutter Hill Company. The Grand Jury wishes to state that the conduct of officials of the Sutter Hill Company is in no way a subject matter of the investigation. They have done nothing of which the Grand Jury is aware that would invite concern. In regard to other parties and participants relative to these transactions there has been some evidence which indicates the possibility of criminal conduct.

- 14 -

However, since a key figure in the transactions, realtor Bruce Morton, cannot be located, the Grand Jury has chosen to take no action and to make no comment concerning its findings at this time.

This concludes the Grand Jury's report.

* * *

In completing its investigation, the Grand Jury wishes to express its appreciation to the special investigative unit of the Washoe County Sheriff's Office headed by Lieutenant Gary Aiazzi. This division of trained investigators has conducted extensive investigation which uncovered valuable evidence later presented to the Grand Jury. The Grand Jury compliments what it finds to be the fine performance of Lieutenant Aiazzi and the men and women of his division.

*Respectfully Submitted*

*Washoe Co. Grand Jury*

*[signature]*

*Foreman*

# APPENDIX B

The following documents chart the journey of Organized Crime Unit Grants from the Law Enforcement
Assitance Administration (LEAA) to Washoe County. Portions of these documents were blanked out in public
documents (which are the versions I have).

( AREA COUNCIL OF GOVERNMENTS (

NOTICE OF INTENT

| Areawide Clearinghouse<br>State Clearinghouse | ESTIMATED APPLICATION FILING DATE<br>APRIL 10, 1974 |
|---|---|

| APPLICANT PROJECT TITLE<br>COUNTY-WIDE ORGANIZED CRIME UNIT | | | |
|---|---|---|---|
| APPLICANT AGENCY<br>WASHOE COUNTY | DIVISION SHERIFF'S DEPARTMENT | | |
| APPLICANT ADDRESS (Street)<br>170 S. SIERRA STREET – P. O. BOX 2915 | CITY<br>RENO | COUNTY<br>WASHOE | ZIPE CODE<br>89505 |
| CONTACT PERSON<br>THOMAS BENHAM, CHIEF DEPUTY | AREA<br>702 | PHONE<br>785-6220 | EXT.<br>260 |
| PROJECT LOCATION-CITY<br>ALL CITIES IN WASHOE COUNTY | PROJECT LOCATION-COUNTY<br>WASHOE COUNTY | | |

PROJECT DESCRIPTION-NATURE, PURPOSE AND BENEFICIARIES (Attach Map and Supporting Documents as Necessary)

This is a request for second year funding of an existing grant, #73-DF-09-0027;

this grant being the County-Wide Organized Crime Unit.

| FEDERAL FUNDS | | MATCHING FUNDS | | OTHER FUNDS | TOTAL FUNDS |
|---|---|---|---|---|---|
| GRANT | OTHER | STATE | LOCAL | | $ 277,349.00 |
| $249,324.00 | | | 28,025.00 | | |

| TYPE OF OTHER FEDERAL FUNDS<br>None | TYPE OF OTHER NON-FEDERAL FUNDS<br>None |
|---|---|

FEDERAL PROGRAMS TITLE AND FEDERAL AID CATALOG NUMBER
OMNIBUS CRIME CONTROL & SAFE STREETS ACT 1968 – FEDERAL AID CATALOG NO. 16.501

| FEDERAL AGENCY NAME<br>U. S. DEPARTMENT OF JUSTICE | FEDERAL SUB-AGENCY: LAW ENFORCEMENT<br>ASSISTANCE ADMINISTRATION |
|---|---|

IS THERE A COMPREHENSIVE PLAN REQUIREMENT?            IS PLAN ON FILE WITH AREAWIDE
                                                     CLEARINGHOUSE

STATE___X___  AREAWIDE_____  LOCAL_____                    Yes   XX

Explain deviations (if any) from pertinent plan (Use back of sheet if necessary)

Is Enviromental Impact Statement or Assessment Required? Yes   No
Does the project involve the relocation or re-establishment of persons, businesses,
farmers or non-profit organizations? Yes   No
Does the Undertaking affect a district, site building, structure or object that is
included in the National Register of Historic Places? Yes   No
If Areawide Clearinghouse is to be notified, fill in date below:
ACOG____APRIL, 1974_____

appendix b

| U. S. DEPARTMENT OF JUSTICE LAW ENFORCEMENT ASSISTANCE ADMINISTRATION | DISCRETIONARY GRANT PROGRESS REPORT | | |
|---|---|---|---|
| GRANTEE Nevada Commission on Crime, Delinquency and Corrections | LEAA GRANT NO. 74-DF-09-0037 | DATE OF REPORT 10-17-75 | REPORT NO. Final |
| IMPLEMENTING SUBGRANTEE Washoe County Sheriff's Department Reno, Nevada | TYPE OF REPORT [x] REGULAR QUARTERLY [ ] SPECIAL REQUEST [x] FINAL REPORT | | |
| SHORT TITLE OF PROJECT County-wide Organized Crime Unit | GRANT AMOUNT $249,324.00 | | |
| REPORT IS SUBMITTED FOR THE PERIOD July 1, 1975 | THROUGH September 15, 1975 | | |
| SIGNATURE OF PROJECT DIRECTOR | TYPED NAME & TITLE OF PROJECT DIRECTOR Thomas F. Benham Chief, Investigative Services Bureau | | |

RECEIVED
OCT 21 1975
Nevada Crime Commission

RECEIVED BY GRANTEE STATE PLANNING AGENCY (Official)

DATE 1/17/76

147

Gordon L. Foote, Chairman, and Representatives on the Council

Frank Freeman, Director

"Notice of Intent" from Washoe County to Apply to the Law Enforcement Assistance Administration for a $249,324 Organized Crime Unit Operational Grant

April 16, 1974

Gentlemen:

Attached for Council consideration is a "Notice of Intent" from Washoe County to apply to the Law Enforcement Assistance Administration for a $249,324 Organized Crime Unit Grant. The total cost of the proposed project is $277,349 with the Federal share amounting to $249,324 and Washoe County's contribution amounting to $28,024.

As Council will recall, at the April 10, 1973, meeting, the Council approved a $258,169 grant request from the Washoe County Sheriff's Department to initiate a County-Wide Organized Crime Unit to undertake the discovery, investigation and evaluation of organized crime within Washoe County and peripheral areas. The proposed project is a request for second year funding of an existing grant program.

The principal goals of the program are:

1. Discovery of organized crime through effective investigation and proper utilization of all legal information sources.

2. Educate, inform, and enlist the community in a continuing program against organized crime.

3. Training of field law enforcement personnel in intelligence methodology suitable to their need and capabilities.

4. Increased prospects of prosecutions successful against organized crime targets.

This project was approved by the Washoe County Planning and Allocations Committee in 1973, and since it is a continuation of an existing program, Mr. Mike Katz, Criminal Justice Planner, informed the A.C.O.G. Office that the Washoe County Planning and Allocations Committee saw no need to review the project again.

The A.C.O.G. Office is aware of no conflicting or duplicating proposals within the project area. Therefore it is recommended that the Council comment favorably on this project and endorse the Washoe County "Notice of Intent" to the Law Enforcement Assistance Administration.

A representative from Sheriff Robert J. Galli's office will be present at the April 18, 1974, Council meeting to answer any questions the Council may have concerning this project.

If you have any questions concerning this agenda item, please do not hesitate to contact me.

Respectfully submitted,

Frank Freeman
Director

FF:blm

cc: Chief Administrator of
Each Member Agency

This final report of Grant No. 74-DF-09-0037 is an
accumulation of activities and accomplishments of the County-
wide Organized Crime Unit occurring during the last fifteen
months of the project.  Our grant extension of three months
accounts for the fifteen months of activity.

## GOAL NUMBER ONE

"Discovery of organized crime through effective investigations and proper utilization of all legal information
sources."

## Accomplishment

Seventy-three investigations of persons, corporations
and/or businesses suspected of being affiliated with principal
organized crime figures were conducted during this grant period.
The disclosed information was disseminated to the appropriate
law enforcement agencies.  All of the collected information
was not prosecutable; however, it provided a greater insight
into the efforts of the syndicated organized crime problem in
northern Nevada.

150

## GOAL NUMBER TWO

"Educate, inform and enlist the community in a continuing program against organized crime."

### Accomplishment

A concerted effort in actively soliciting the community in a program against organized crime has not been initiated. A public awareness program has been designed that will satisfy this goal. The program is scheduled to be implemented during the next grant period; however, a practical approach in satisfying the goal was used. Local community groups have requested presentations from the unit on the local organized crime problem. These requests were generated by the news media coverage of the Grand Jury's governmental corruption inquiries. The information could not be revealed; however, the history of organized crime and its current trends were the topics related to by the speaker.

## GOAL NUMBER THREE

"Information exchange through a centralized group capable of evaluating and interpreting such data."

### Accomplishment

The raw data supplied to the unit by its own investigators and other law enforcement agencies is accurately evaluated and properly disseminated to the appropriate jurisdictions. Other law enforcement agencies are encouraged to request assistance from the Organized Crime Unit in collecting information. This affords the opportunity for a free flow of information between agencies, and we are made aware of certain criminals in our jurisdiction. The unit served as a centralized coordinator for both in-state and out-of-state law enforcement agencies while conducting approximately fifty-three investigations at the request of various outside agencies.

The following example will illustrate only one of the accomplishments of the unit:

GOAL NUMBER FOUR

"Training of field law enforcement personnel in intelligence methodology suitable to their needs and capabilities."

Accomplishment

The investigators assigned to the Organized Crime Unit have all received training in the collection of information, handling of informants, development of witnesses, and the proper dissemination of analyzed data. Some of this training was conducted in a classroom while other training was on-the-job by the unit supervisors.

Law enforcement personnel of the Washoe County Sheriff's Department assigned to the Patrol Division have attended special training sessions presented by supervisors of the Organized Crime Unit. Additionally, patrolmen have worked with unit investigators on specific targets in areas where they were knowledgeable.

GOAL NUMBER FIVE

"Increased prospects of successful prosecutions against organized crime."

AR   COUNCIL OF GOVERNMENTS   (

TO:     Robert Rusk, Chairman, and Representatives on the
        Council,

FROM:   Frank Freeman, Director

SUBJECT:    "Notice of Intent" from Washoe County to apply
            to the U. S. Department of Justice for a
            $185,520 Organized Crime Prevention Program
            Grant.

March 29, 1973

Gentlemen:

Attached for Council consideration is a "Notice of Intent"
from Washoe County to apply to the U. S. Department of Justice
for a $185,520 Organized Crime Prevention Program Grant.  The
total cost of the proposed project is estimated to be $258,196
with the Federal Share amounting to $185,520, and Washoe
County's contribution amounting to $72,676.

The proposed project basically consists of developing a
single unit approach to the discovery, investigation, and
evaluation of organized crime within Washoe County and its
peripheral areas.

The principal goals of the Program are:

    1.  Discovery of Organized Crime through effective inves-
        tigation and proper utilization of all legal informa-
        tion sources.

    2.  Educate, inform, and enlist the community in a con-
        tinuing program against organized crime.

    3.  Training of field law enforcement personnel in In-
        telligence methodology suitable to their need and
        capabilities.

    4.  Increased prospects of prosecutions successful against
        Organized Crime Targets.

This Project has been approved by the Washoe County Alloca-
tions Committee, which is the Areawide Law Enforcement
Planning Committee, and the Washoe County Board of County
Supervisors.

The C.O.G. office is aware of no conflicting or duplicating
proposals within the Project, therefore, it is recommended
that the Council comment favorably and endorse Washoe County's
"Notice of Intent" to the U. S. Justice Department.

A representative of Sheriff Robert V. Galli's office will be
present at the April 10, 1973 Council Meeting to answer any

-1-

Item 4

questions which the Council may have concerning this Project.

If you have any questions pertaining to the attached "Notice of Intent", please do not hesitate to contact me.

Respectively submitted,

FRANK FREEMAN, Director

FF:G
CC:Chief Administrator of
all Member Agencies

-2-

155

| U. S. DEPARTMENT OF JUSTICE<br>LAW ENFORCEMENT ASSISTANCE ADMINISTRATION | DISCRETIONARY GRANT<br>PROGRESS REPORT | | |
|---|---|---|---|
| GRANTEE<br>NEVADA COMMISSION ON CRIME,<br>DELINQUENCY & CORRECTIONS | LEAA GRANT NO.<br>76-DF-09-0003 | DATE OF REPORT<br>1-9-76 | REPORT NO.<br>2nd Qtr. |
| IMPLEMENTING SUBGRANTEE<br>WASHOE COUNTY SHERIFF'S DEPARTMENT<br>RENO, NEVADA | TYPE OF REPORT<br>☒ REGULAR QUARTERLY ☐ SPECIAL REQUEST<br>☐ FINAL REPORT | | |
| SHORT TITLE OF PROJECT<br>COUNTY-WIDE ORGANIZED CRIME UNIT | GRANT AMOUNT<br>$197,651.00 | | |
| REPORT IS SUBMITTED FOR THE PERIOD | THROUGH March 31, 1976 | | |
| SIGNATURE OF PROJECT DIRECTOR | TYPED NAME & TITLE OF PROJECT DIRECTOR<br>THOMAS F. BENHAM<br>CHIEF, INVESTIGATIVE SERVICES BUREAU | | |

COMMENCE REPORT HERE (Add continuation pages as required.)

(SEE ATTACHED REPORT)

RECEIVED
STATE OF NEVADA

APR 19 1976

CRIME COMMISSION
CARSON CITY, NEVADA

CONFIDENTIAL
Not Subject To
Public Inspection

RECEIVED BY GRANTEE/STATE PLANNING AGENCY (Official)

DATE 4-19-76

LEAA FORM 4527/1 (REV 1-73)     REPLACES LEAA-OLEP-152, WHICH IS OBSOLETE.     DOJ--1973--05

This quarterly report reveals a portion of the activities and accomplishments of the County-wide Organized Crime Unit from January 1, 1976 through March 31, 1976. The report does not reveal information concerning sensitive investigations; however, it should be considered a confidential report.

Nevada Task Force, comprised of four agencies, has been formed to assist in the endeavor. The task force is anticipated to be operational during the next quarter. Hopefully, the task force will be beneficial to the state as a whole in monitoring the criminal elements movement.

GOAL NUMBER TWO

"Educate, inform and enlist the community in a continuing program against organized crime."

The achievement of this goal was accomplished by various means during the past quarter. The most significant method was the release of a Washoe County Grand Jury report which enlisted the community's support in a campaign for good government. The local press strongly attacked the problems of political corruption which resulted in considerable correspondence between the citizens of the community and the local editors of the news media. A television poll revealed the public was aroused by the news contained in the Grand Jury report; exposure was favored four-to-one.

3.

Those people named in the report have criticized the
Washoe County Grand Jury, the Washoe County District Attorney's
Office, and the Washoe County Sheriff's Department, Organized
Crime Unit. Their criticism prompted a limited amount of disclosure of the Organized Crime Unit's efforts within Washoe
County. Invitations were accepted and presentations were made
to audiences of high school members, a journalism class of the
University of Nevada, members of the United States Naval Reserve,
and local civic organizations. The theme of the Project
Director's presentations was cost of the Organized Crime Unit
versus the amount of dollars impact upon the community. The
program was limited to twenty investigations conducted by the
unit that clearly revealed a monetary value. This limited
equation represents total unit cost of approximately $700,000.00
and an impact upon the community in excess of $2,000,000.00.
The disclosures achieved even greater community support for
the continuance of the Organized Crime Unit on the local level.

GOAL NUMBER THREE

"Information exchange through a centralized group capable
of evaluating and interpreting such data."

As verified in the "Summary of Investigations" section
of this report, satisfaction of this goal was achieved during
the quarter. The grant file contains many letters of appreciation from various agencies regarding cases investigated by the
unit's detectives. An accounting of the contacts with other
police agencies for the purposes of information exchange is too

4.

lengthy to list. The exchange of evaluated information has resulted in the initiation of new investigations within Washoe
County and other jurisdictions.

GOAL NUMBER FOUR

"Training of field law enforcement personnel in intelligence methodology suitable to their needs and capabilities."

Training was provided to one unit detective in the field
of technical surveillance equipment from the National Intelligence
Academy. A specialized slot machine cheating seminar was held
for three unit detectives in conjunction with the newly formed
Northern Nevada Gaming Task Force. Various organized crime related books have been purchased and cataloged into the unit's
library; the books are required reading material for the unit's
members.

GOAL NUMBER FIVE

"Increased prospects of successful prosecutions against
organized crime."

On March 15, 1976, the Washoe County Grand Jury issued a
report to the general public of Washoe County. (Report attached).
The report exposed an attempt by an organized crime figure to in-
filtrate governmental bodies within Washoe County. The problems
of political corruption, the need for stronger controls on governmental bodies, more stringent health requirements on legalized
prostitution in adjoining counties, and the need for revised anti-
conflict of interest legislation were covered in the report.

Legislative reform has been publicly suggested by some

5.

legislators and the news media. The sincerity of the suggestions cannot be determined until the close of the next legislative session.

NOTIFICATION OF INTENT TO APPLY FOR FEDERAL AID

| Applicant | | | Department |
|---|---|---|---|
| WASHOE COUNTY | | | SHERIFF |

| Applicant Address | Street | City | Zip |
|---|---|---|---|
| P. O. Box 2915 | | Reno, Nevada | 89505 |

| Contact Person | | Area Code | Phone | Ext. |
|---|---|---|---|---|
| ROBERT J. GALLI, SHERIFF | | 702 | 785-6220 | 89431 Zip |

Project Title

ORGANIZED CRIME PREVENTION PROGRAM

| Project Location | City | County |
|---|---|---|

WASHOE COUNTY                                    WASHOE COUNTY

Project Description  (If necessary attach supporting Documents)

The proposed Project basically consists of developing a single

unit approach to the discovery and investigation of Organized

Crime within Washoe County.

| Federal Funds | | Non-Federal Matching Funds | |
|---|---|---|---|
| (A) Grant | (B) Other | (C) State | (D) Local |
| $185,520 | | | $72,676 |

Federal Program Title

OMNIBUS CRIME CONTROL AND SAFE STREETS ACT

| Federal Agency Name | Federal Sub-Agency Name |
|---|---|
| U. S. DEPT. OF JUSTICE | LAW ENFORCEMENT ASSISTANCE ADMIN. |

TYPE OF APPLICANT:
        Inter-                                        School    Special
State_____ State_____ County_ X ___ City_____ District District___

IS THERE A COMPREHENSIVE PLAN?

State_ X ___ Trhionsl_ X ___ Local_____

ESTIMATED APPLICATION FILING DATE:  Month_ 4 __ Day_ 15 __ Year___ 1973

I. FEDERAL CATALOG NO. (OR PUBLIC LAW NO. & TITLE)___ 1968 _____
      PUBLIC LAW 90-351 As Amended in 1970
II. HAS METROPOLITAN CLEARINGHOUSE BEEN NOTIFIED? (ACOG) 3/19/73 Date
III.HAS FUNDING AGENCY BEEN NOTIFIED? Yes X No    Feb. 1973 Date
IV. IF PROJECT INCLUDES STATE FUNDS, IDENTIFY AGENCY_____

V. LIST PERTINENT PLANNING DOCUMENTS OR PROJECT STUDIES_____

| U. S. DEPARTMENT OF JUSTICE LAW ENFORCEMENT ASSISTANCE ADMINISTRATION | DISCRETIONARY GRANT PROGRESS REPORT | | |
|---|---|---|---|
| **GRANTEE** NEVADA COMMISSION ON CRIME, DELINQUENCY & CORRECTIONS | **LEAA GRANT NO.** 76-DF-09-0003 | **DATE OF REPORT** 7-9-76 | **REPORT NO.** 3rd Qtr. |
| **IMPLEMENTING SUBGRANTEE** WASHOE COUNTY SHERIFF'S DEPT. RENO, NEVADA | **TYPE OF REPORT** [X] REGULAR QUARTERLY [ ] SPECIAL REQUEST [ ] FINAL REPORT | | |
| **SHORT TITLE OF PROJECT** COUNTY-WIDE ORGANIZED CRIME UNIT | **GRANT AMOUNT** $197,651.00 | | |

REPORT IS SUBMITTED FOR THE PERIOD March 31, 1976 THROUGH June 30, 1976

**SIGNATURE OF PROJECT DIRECTOR**

**TYPED NAME & TITLE OF PROJECT DIRECTOR**
THOMAS F. BENHAM
Chief, Investigative Services Bureau

COMMENCE REPORT HERE (Add continuation pages as required.)

(See attached report)

REGION IX

| | |
|---|---|
| RA | |
| DOPS | |
| CA-NV | |
| AZ | |
| HI-GU-HS | |
| PIE | |
| OR | |
| CONTROL | |
| M | |
| J | |
| JUV-SYS | |
| LE-P-MAN | |
| FRO-CTS | |
| DMH | |
| FS | |
| ADMIN | |
| SEC | |

RECEIVED BY GRANTEE STATE PLANNING AGENCY (Official)

DATE

LEAA FORM 4587/1 (REV. 1-73)    REPLACES LEAA-OLEP-159, WHICH IS OBSOLETE.    DOJ-1973-

This quarterly report reveals only a portion of the activities and accomplishments of the County-wide Organized Crime Unit from March 31, 1976 through June 30, 1976. The report does not disclose sensitive information; however, it should be considered a confidential report.

## GOAL NUMBER ONE

"Discovery of organized crime through effective investigations and proper utilization of all legal information sources."

The period of time this report covers did not reveal any unknown organized crime figures. A large portion of the unit's efforts was devoted to the updating of information on visiting organized crime persons previously discovered. Our conclusion is the visits were for business purposes rather than entertainment.

interest from the Attorney General's Office. The United States Postal Authority Inspectors will be informed of our investigation pending a mutual meeting date.

## LABOR UNION ACTIVITIES

There were no reported or discovered improper union activities during this period.

## CONTROLLED SUBSTANCES REFERRALS

Four new narcotics investigations were referred to the appropriate enforcement agencies during the quarter.

## GOAL NUMBER TWO

"Educate, inform and enlist the community in a continuing program against organized crime."

2.

Through efforts to discover new organized crime activities, we became familiar with the carnival concession business. The major concern was with the financial structure of some of the larger carnival shows frequenting Washoe County. Results of our inquiries revealed a need to inform the community of the ever present possibility of rigged games for the purpose of cheating the public.

Our first opportunity to enlighten the public was on May 22nd and May 23rd at the Washoe County Criminal Justice Planners Committee Law and Order Days. The program, entitled "Community Awareness Presentation", enabled the public to participate in actual "rigged" games at no cost to the individuals. Unit detectives enacted the parts of concessionaires in two carnival booths and a slide presentation was visible. Each booth contained a large variety of commonly "rigged" carnival games. A single page handout, provided to interested parties, depicted some indicators of rigged games. (Refer to Attachment A). There was a favorable response from the public; and their most common question was, "Why aren't you doing something about it?" We advised everyone that in this particular area, we do intend to recommend and support new regulatory laws during the next legislative session. There were some personal pledges made to contact Nevada lawmakers. Since the Law Day presentation, the department has been invited to participate in five other instructional demonstrations. (Refer to Attachment B, Visual Display).

3.

Our endeavors have opened a new avenue to informing and enlist-
ing the community in a continuing program against organized
crime. Equipment used in the demonstrations were modeled from
rigged games that had been confiscated by California authorities. These games were made by the unit's detectives on their
own time and have been donated to the Washoe County Sheriff's
Department.

In summary, the "Community Awareness Presentation" was a success
from many different standpoints.

1. Law enforcement benefited as a whole from the
   favorable exposure to the community.

2. The public was made aware of the large amounts
   of money that changes hands during a two or three
   day visit to a community by a carnival.

3. Some community support was received for new
   legislation to combat one form of organized
   crime income in this state.

GOAL NUMBER THREE

"Information exchange through a centralized group capable of
evaluating and interpreting such data."

Information is being exchanged on a daily basis with other law
enforcement agencies.

GOAL NUMBER FOUR

"Training of field law enforcement personnel in intelligence
methodology suitable to their needs and capabilities."

4.

Specialized training programs were not conducted or attended during this quarter.

Re: BIGLIERI, SHIRLEY M.

To Whom It May Concern:

I am writing this letter at the request of Mr. Clyde Biglieri, in follow-up of my previous communication of July 30, 2001. I have followed Shirley Biglieri since 1987 for the problems of paroxysmal atrial fibrillation, associated with hypertensive cardiovascular disease, associated with mild aortic and mitral valve disease, and then the subsequent development of coronary heart disease requiring bypass grafting, and then ultimately the cardiovascular problems associated with her subsequent development of cancer.

Mr. Biglieri has asked specifically for me to comment on whether or not Mrs. Biglieri ever mentioned the stress of the situation regarding his legal difficulties during her follow-up. The answer is that she did. I saw her in 1987 through 1989 and during that time she described significant anxiety and stress and sleep disturbance, which she attributed to Mr. Biglieri's legal dispute. I cannot prove cause or relationship between this and her hypertension or state whether or not she would have had hypertension without it, but it is unquestionably true that she mentioned the problem on every visit during those occasions. The focus of my notes is on the cardiovascular problems, of course, but I believe the notes of 4/14/87, and 11/8/89 do list the problem of her significant chronic anxiety and stress resulting from this. Obviously, the focus of our interaction in the late 1990s when I began seeing her again was the nature of her grave medical problems during those times and therefore did not focus so much on the problems of her stress and anxiety as the notes had previously described, because by then the severity of her medical problems had completely overshadowed any other consideration.

# Goodnight, Shirley.

**IN LOVING MEMORY**

## Shirley M. Biglieri

Nov. 27, 1928 to May 27, 2001

*Thanksgiving and your birthday,*
*How perfect! One of the blessings*
*we're most thankful for is our*
*wonderful parents! We miss you so,*
*Mama.*

*Your Girls*